The Mirror of Nature

Miss Louisa Fairbrother as Aladdin in *The Forty Thieves*

Robertson Davies

THE
MIRROR
OF NATURE

The Alexander Lectures

1982

University of Toronto Press

Toronto Buffalo London

©University of Toronto Press 1983
Toronto Buffalo London
Printed in Canada
ISBN 0-8020-6536-8

Publication of this book
is made possible by grants from
University College, University of Toronto,
and from the Canada Council and
the Ontario Arts Council
under their block grant programs.

Canadian Cataloguing in Publication Data

Davies, Robertson, 1913-
The mirror of nature
(The Alexander lectures, ISSN 0065-616x ; 1982)
ISBN 0-8020-6536-8
1. English drama – 19th century – History and criticism –
Addresses, essays, lectures.
2. Theater – England – History – 19th century –
Addresses, essays, lectures.
I. Title. II. Series.

PR733.D38   822'.8   C83-098475-5

Mr Principal, Ladies, and Gentlemen

I account it a great honour to have been asked to deliver these lectures, and before I begin I wish to pay special homage to the memory of Professor William John Alexander, in whose honour, and to perpetuate whose memory, they were founded.

Professor Alexander exercised an incalculable influence on education in this country, especially by means of the anthology he prepared for use in high schools, called *Shorter Poems*. It was in its pages that I, like hundreds of thousands of other young Canadians, learned a great deal about the pleasures of verse, and especially of Canadian poetry, of which the book contained a large and carefully chosen selection. It was through Professor Alexander, whom I never saw or heard, that I nevertheless learned that Canada had poets, and good ones.

Contents

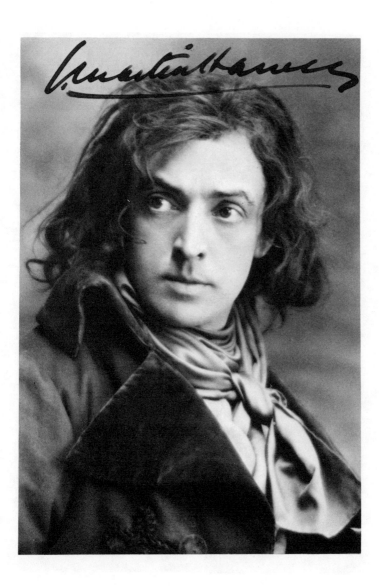

Mr Martin Harvey as *Rouget De Lisle*

Mr E.A. Sothern as Lord Dundreary in *Our American Cousin*

Mr Edwin Booth as Richelieu

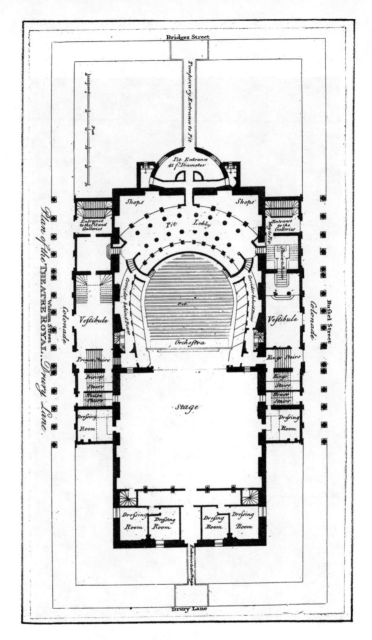

floor plan of Drury Lane Theatre

Miss Scott as *Black Ey'd Susan*

M. Victorien Sardou,
author of *La Tosca, Madame Sans-Gene,* etc

LECTURE ONE

Oblivion's Balm

IN THESE LECTURES I hope that I may persuade you to look with imaginative sympathy at a realm of dramatic writing that has, until recently, been treated with neglect and sometimes with scorn. The drama of the nineteenth century, which was utterly ignored by scholars when I was an undergraduate – indeed an object of mockery if by chance it happened to be mentioned – has, during the past fifty years, become of interest to students of the history of the theatre – which is itself a study of comparatively recent growth.

When I was an undergraduate it was the academic custom to assure students that the theatre of the mind was a vastly finer place for the realization of the plays of Shakespeare, and indeed for any drama of literary worth, than was the playhouse. But all that has changed, and I think that in part the change is owing to the fact that our century has been a particularly rich period in the art of acting, and the new art of play production has thrown a new light on many kinds of drama. These arts – acting and play-direction – have learned a great deal from the world of literary criticism, and conversely – beginning perhaps with the scholarly and theatrically informed writing of Harley Granville-Barker – have shown that the playhouse has much of value to teach the scholarly world. And thus a gap has been bridged, to the advantage of both stage and university.

It is not my intention, however, to recapitulate the historical work that has been done on the nineteenth-century theatre by such scholars as Michael Booth, George Rowell, and Richard Southern, to name but three. Nor do I propose to travel once again the path so dauntlessly cleared by Allardyce Nicoll, who showed us how much nineteenth-century drama there was, what its principal concerns were, and, in broad outline, how well those concerns were served. He it was, more than any other, who made it possible to survey critically what had for so long been dismissed as a tangle unworthy of being straightened out. We can now see that, although the nineteenth century has little of literary worth to offer in its theatre, it provides a counterpoint to the greater literature of the century, and is in itself an absorbing study in the psychology of the era.

So you see that it is not history or literary criticism to which I propose to turn your attention, for I have nothing of special consequence to add to what has already been done. What I bring is speculation on a theme which I approach with no complete confidence that I can explore it fully, but which I attempt because so far as I know it has not been explored in quite this way before.

What I hope to do is to examine the theatre of the nineteenth century, to show the change in psychological bias that took place during the century, and to try to throw some light on how people in general – not the scholars or the leaders of opinion, but the mass of the population – came to think of themselves. What was it that made the minds of so many ordinary citizens in 1900 very different from the minds of their counterparts in 1800? Who did this new sort of person think he was, what were his expectations from life, and in what relationship did he stand toward the rest of his kind? I shall draw my material from the drama of one hundred years, because I regard the theatre as a Mirror of Nature, and that is why I have given that title to this group of lectures.

Everybody knows the phrase. It comes from *Hamlet*, where the Prince of Denmark, himself theatre-struck – in a half-academic, half-amateur way – undertakes to instruct a company of professional actors – having been told that they are the best actors in the world – in the rudiments of their art. Hamlet speaks of 'the purpose of playing, whose end, both at the first and now, was and is, to hold, as 'twere, the mirror up to nature; to show virtue her own feature, scorn her own image, and the very age and body of the time his form and pressure.'

Admirable general advice, and of course capable of many interpretations. The moderate take it as a counsel of moderation, with results that are not always fortunate, for the moderation of the great artist is by no means the moderation of timidity or ineptitude. Whenever Realism is in fashion, it is sometimes used to bring in Shakespeare as a witness on behalf of Realism, meaning a faithful imitation of the externals of dramatic action. As a theatrical mode Realism has its qualities, but its severe limitations as well, and Shakespeare was far too much an artist to have had much use for it. He would have agreed with Goethe that art is art because it is not nature. I suggest that in analysing the phrase we should not be solely occupied with the word 'mirror,' which is static in its suggestion, but give appropriate emphasis to 'nature,' which is widely variable. What do you suppose Shakespeare meant by 'nature'?

Did he not mean that which is recognizable and acceptable by an audience – that which commands assent and belief, that which speaks not merely to the eye, which can recognize the external form of things, but speaks rather to the spirit of the hearer? 'Nature' as it applies to art is not a word of fixed and immutable meaning. 'Nature' surely is what people apprehend as true to life as they know it, and not to the outward forms of life only but to the heart and – if I may use a four-letter word that many people find objectionable – to the soul?

The play Hamlet asks the players to perform has not much of external 'nature' in it for a modern audience, and the dumb-show that preceded it was old-fashioned and therefore unlikely to seem natural to an audience in 1600. But *The Mousetrap* (Shakespeare was first to use that too-familiar title) holds the mirror up to the inner nature of Claudius and Gertrude, and thus it convinces us that it has reached its mark. What is, at that moment in the Danish court, most significant in the form and pressure of the time, or as we might say its psychological climate, is shown in the play. By means far from realistic, psychological truth has been evoked.

I hope to show that this is true, in greater or less degree, in all plays that gain a hold in public acceptance. Not all are as bald in their declaration as *The Mousetrap*, but they show the form and pressure of the time, and the underlying state of mind of the audiences that welcome them. It is this state of mind which is of uttermost importance if we hope to gain a sympathetic understanding of any age. It is not, of course, something that the age itself defines, or anatomizes, or discusses because it is an apparently incoherent mass of prejudices, notions, and generally accepted attitudes. It is that which most people, at a given time, take for granted as so obvious that it needs no explanation or defence.

In the theatre, where people of widely different attainments in education, culture, and social status are gathered whenever a play is presented, this underlying body of belief, fear, and aspiration is clearly and sometimes coarsely or naively displayed. Not so in poetry, which has always – since the invention of printing – been for those who wish to plunge below the surface of superficial feelings. Not so in the novel, which by its very form invites psychological probing, and the presentation of more than one point of view. Poetry and the novel are encountered by the solitary reader, drawn apart from his fellows. But a play must make its effect immediately, in a short time, on a mixed audience whose attention must be seized and held from distraction, and that expects qualities for its money which do not trouble poetry or the novel. So, if the theatre is shallow, what is it banishing to the depths? If it is a theatre of thrills and marvels, what compensations do these offer to its auditors? If the theatre is falsely jocose about such a subject as sex, what fear is being dispelled in laughter? In the theatre of the nineteenth century the lights in the auditorium were not turned low during the performance, and the measure of privacy we enjoy in modern theatres was not therefore available; for this reason, to be present in the theatre was to condone, in some measure, what was done on the stage, as one need not condone the poem or the novel read in solitude. To be present in an audience is still, in our time, somewhat to condone the performance. We are claiming to be at one with the players as we do not need to admit to being at one with the poet or the novelist.

Remember, too, that in the nineteenth century the theatre supplied the demand for entertainment of the dramatic sort that is now shared among the stage, the film, and television, and was to that extent very much the only mirror of nature. And what was nature? What was taken for granted, or feared, or fiercely desired? What was the psychological background of the century?

By the year 1800 the psychological change we call the Romantic Movement was well under way, and reaching from the intellectual level where it had its genesis outward through the whole of society. It would be possible to spend all of these three lectures attempting to define what the Romantic Movement was, but in briefest psychological terms it meant a turning inward, and a preoccupation with particularities of personal feeling, as opposed to the Neo-Classical attitude of generalization and conventional acceptance which dominated so much thought during the eighteenth century. The poet, said Samuel Johnson, did not number the streaks of the tulip, or describe the different shades of verdure of the forest. But under the spell of Romanticism that was precisely what the poet did; he made the tulip and the forest his own, and he offered his readers what was most individual about his personal vision, rather than what might be assumed to be common to mankind.

In religion, the struggle of the individual soul toward its salvation was at the root of the Evangelical Movement which is akin to Romanticism. Under Romantic influence, everybody was possessed of a soul that was his own and held in trust for God. What this religious revival meant politically brought about a revolution more profound than the violent overthrow in France. Of course a sense of being a man, and having feelings that must be respected, was nothing new, and the eighteenth century had known it well. But what was usually meant by that state of mind was being a *laudable* man and having *laudable* feelings. Under the Romantic spell it became permissible and almost preferable to have highly particularized feelings, some of which might appear to society to be eccentric and even reprehensible.

In Lord Byron we encounter a figure divided between eighteenth-century attitudes and those of the new age. In a letter to Tom Moore this aristocratic poet described Wordsworth as 'that pedlar-praising son of a bitch' (*Letters*, volume 11, p 198) because he disliked Wordsworth's enthusiasm for what we now call the Common Man; like so many people who claim special consideration for idiosyncracies of their own, Byron was not ready to believe that such feelings existed, or should be encouraged, among the lower orders. When, in his novel *Sybil*, Disraeli spoke of 'Two nations, between whom there is no intercourse and no sympathy; who are as ignorant of each other's habits, thoughts and feelings as if they were dwellers in different zones, or inhabitants of different planets; who are formed by a different breeding, are fed by a different food, are ordered by different manners, and are not governed by the same laws,' he spoke of the rich and the poor, and of a situation which the tide of Romantic feeling was sweeping away. Nowhere was this change more immediately and startlingly obvious than in the theatre, where the new feeling was presented sometimes coarsely, sometimes with painful timidity, always in terms that were comprehensible to audiences where many playgoers might be illiterate and many more were ignorant, but presented with an insistence that gives the theatre a special importance as an agent of social change, and particularly of psychological change, for society and its psychology are inextricably linked. The drama was not eager to be an agent of this change; it merely said what its audiences wanted to hear, and what they wanted to hear was that in the realm of emotion there were not two nations but one, and that in love and hate, in all the deep concerns of life, Jack was as good as his master and quite possibly better. And how did it do that? It is part of my task to consider that question.

The protest is not a political or economic one; it is Romantically individual. We can uncover plenty of plays about mutinies at sea, or strikes in factories, or about the wretched lot of the climbing boys who worked pretty much as slaves for chimney sweeps, but when we put them together they appear not as social protest, but as the determination of individuals to seek redress for personal wrongs. In the immensely popular *Black Eyed Susan* (Surrey Theatre, 1829) the noble sailor is protesting not against inhumane conditions in the Navy but because his captain has laid seige to his wife. In *The Factory Lad* (Surrey Theatre, 1832) the action concentrates on Will Rushton, a single victim of injustice, rather than on the many who suffer the cruelty of the mill-owner who replaces them with steam-driven machines.

Sometimes it is said that this bias of nineteenth-century drama is owing to the fact that the censorship would not have tolerated plays of social protest. I know this to be true in part, but I think that the stronger reason for the concentration on a single figure was that for the first time in his history the labourer, the farm-hand, or the factory operative, was emerging into a new conception of himself as a being differentiated from the mass. It is not his economic, but his emotional, sufferings that are stressed, and he is a distinguished figure among his fellow sailors, or fellow workers, or whatever they may be – a man with stronger, finer feelings than theirs, and a command of rhetoric that can make his troubles appear to be of commanding importance.

Nineteenth-century rhetoric is heady stuff, and deserves more attention than I shall be able to give it. One of the perennial problems of the playwright is how to make his inarticulate characters present their thoughts persuasively without violating probability. It is a problem that gave immense trouble to, for instance, Eugene O'Neill, who grew up, let us remember, in the bosom of the theatre of Melodrama. The nineteenth-century playwright solved the problem by flinging probability to the winds. Thus, in *The Factory Lad*, Will Rushton strikes down his oppressor, crying, 'Spurn a helpless and imploring woman, whose heart is broken – whose mind is crazed? If *her* voice is weak, my *arm* is not. Justice shall have its due. Die, tyrant! Quick, to where water quencheth not!' He shoots the mill-owner and as the curtain falls he is laughing hysterically. This is industrial unrest as seen in the mirror of nature, rather than on television news.

Listen to what William, the simple sailor in *Black Eyed Susan*, says when he sets foot ashore, to greet his darling wife: 'Huzza, huzza! My noble fellows, my heart jumps like a dolphin – my head turns round like a capstern; I feel as if I were driving before the gale of pleasure for the haven of joy.'

And when it is pointed out to him that Susan has not come to meet him, he rejoins: 'Why, no! that is, you see, because we dropped anchor afore the poor things had turned out of their hammocks. Ah! if my Susan knew who was here, she'd soon lash and carry, roused up by the whistle of that young boatswain's mate, Cupid, piping in her heart.' The humble nineteenth-century playgoer went to the theatre to hear people like himself talking not as he talked but rather as he would talk if it lay within his power. Will Rushton and Sweet William romanticise the Common Man by giving him a golden tongue.

This was not solely a theatrical convention. Dickens' humble characters are often extremely rhetorical; see how Thackeray makes his footmen talk in *The Yellowplush Papers*; read the conversations of people of humble life in the novels of Harrison Ainsworth and Henry Cockton. Dickens can make a humble clerk like Dick Swiveller say, 'Fan the sinking flame of hilarity with the wing of friendship; and pass the rosy wine.' Where did Dick learn to talk like that? In the theatre, probably. But when Dick says: 'I never nursed a dear Gazelle, to glad me with its soft black eye, but when it came to know me well, and love me, it was sure to marry a market gardener,' he is adapting a popular portion of Tom Moore's *Lalla Rookh* to his own situation; his beloved has jilted him for a low fellow named Cheggles. And where did Dick learn that, do you suppose? Perhaps we shall come to that later. But all the evidence we have suggests that the common man endeavoured, when he could, to speak above a mortal mouth.

Dickens was not deluded by the notion that when people in humble life attempted rhetoric they always twanged it off with the real theatrical adeptness. Listen to this rhetorical exchange, which has a strong ring of probability about it, from *Little Dorrit*: ' "John Edward Nandy," said Mr Plornish, addressing the old gentleman, "Sir. It's not too often that you see unpretending actions without a spark of pride, and therefore when you see them, give grateful honour unto the same, being that if you don't and live to want 'em it follows serve you right." To which Mr Nandy heartily replied: "I am heartily of your opinion, Thomas, and which your opinion is the same as mine, and therefore no more words, and not being backward with that opinion, which that opinion giving it as yes, Thomas, yes, in the opinion in which yourself and me must be unanimously jined by all, and where there is not difference of opinion there can be none but one opinion, which fully no, Thomas, Thomas, no!" '

This, in its aspiring ineptitude is not theatrical rhetoric, but theatrical rhetoric is at its root.

The rhetoric of the nineteenth century is not an ignoble mode of expression. The modern prejudice in favour of simplicity of speech and writing is pretty much an upper-class, educated-class affair, but even the most austere among us is likely to be moved by poetry when it rises to splendour, and by rhetoric too, which is what Edward Thomas calls 'the imitation of poetic intensity' – sometimes no bad imitation. Almost anything is preferable to a creeping lowness of utterance, like a television drama clawing blindly in the ragbag of colloquial speech for something that will serve to evoke emotion.

In the nineteenth century everybody seems to have employed as much rhetoric as he could command, from the astonishing public addresses of Macaulay and Gladstone to the conversation, often skilfully rhetorical, of the humblest, as recorded by Mayhew in *London Labour and the London Poor* (1851-61).

The power of nineteenth-century rhetoric has been splendidly vindicated in the Royal Shakespeare Company's nine-hour drama of *Nicholas Nickleby* (1980) at which audiences responded with an enthusiasm rarely seen in the theatre to language and situation far removed from the commonplace of modern life but close and responsive to modern feeling. We are now far enough from the nineteenth century to see its excesses and its virtues, and to find what concerns ourselves in both. Beneath these excesses and among these virtues we find the psychological atmosphere of the nineteenth century and, if we do not share it, we can understand and perhaps sympathize with it.

Those of you who are already familiar with the appearance and mechanics of the nineteenth-century theatre will, I hope, pardon me if for a moment I say something about matters which are necessary if nineteenth-century drama is to be understood, even in modest measure. First of all, it was a beautiful theatre. The decor was by no means the gaudy scarlet and gold we see in theatres that were built toward the end of the century: the usual colour scheme was fawn and green, touched here and there with gold; the shape was the horseshoe we still see in the older opera houses, with tiers of galleries hanging steeply from the walls, so that even the cheapest seats were reasonably near the stage; there were private boxes for the well-to-do, the pit for the middle class, and galleries for the poor. The proscenium was a beautiful picture-frame, but in front of it projected a forestage of considerable area, and it could be entered by two proscenium doors, which were also incorporated into whatever scene appeared on the open stage; it was one of the conventions of this theatre that when, perhaps, a rocky mountain pass was presented on the stage characters might enter or escape through one of these doors, even though it looked like a door in a palace or a handsome public building. This was not a realistic theatre.

Technically it was by no means a naive theatre. Theatrical invention was as high as it has ever been; scene-painting was splendid in the magnificent but not wholly realistic interiors and exteriors it could present; the stage was surrounded by a mass of invisible machinery that enabled demons to come up through the floor, angels to descend from the sky; ghosts to manifest themselves anywhere; real water to flow, and fire to break out realistically wherever it was wanted. All of this machinery was designed to move the action along at top speed, by an elaborate device of stage grooves enabling one scene to succeed another by the opening of shutter-like screens, so that the action proceeded by a series of what film or television call 'dissolves.' A film-like speed could be achieved, and there were no waits while scenes were changed. In all these matters the nineteenth-century theatre had a sophistication that many modern theatres might envy.

There were limitations. Lighting, depending on candles, or oil lamps, and later gas, would look dim to us today, especially as the lights in the auditorium were never lowered; it was Henry Irving who introduced that refinement late in the century. The theatres could be hot and stuffy as the long program, beginning at six o'clock and going on until midnight, took its course. People flirted, talked, and ate in the boxes; people flirted, talked, and ate in the galleries. Rowdy interruptions were not uncom-

mon if the play did not please. Applause was frequent, and an admired delivery of a well-known
speech (a soliloquy of Hamlet's, for instance) or a
splendid patriotic or manly sentiment brought a
round of applause like that we now hear in an opera
house when a singer distinguishes himself. I have
examined the plans of many of these theatres carefully, and I cannot find any lavatory accommoda-
tion for the audience whatever, although a full
evening's performance might last for six hours, so
there was a good deal of coming and going. At nine
o'clock admission to the theatres was reduced to
half-price and at that time, whatever might be hap-
pening on the stage, crowds of city clerks invaded
the house, looked for vacant seats, and apparently
made a good deal of noise. The respectful silence,
amounting sometimes almost to stupor, that we find
in a modern theatre was unknown.

Acting, therefore, had to be broad and authori-
tative, and the actors had voices that could dominate
unruly crowds. John Gielgud tells a story of his
uncle Fred Terry, the inheritor of a century-long
tradition of the Terry golden utterance, on an occasion when he was rehearsing what was supposed
to be an angry crowd. Finally, in despair, he re-
quested all the ladies to go to the Green Room, and
then he addressed his unsatisfactory rioters.
'Gentlemen,' he said, 'I could fart louder than that.'
The tradition of these splendid voices – and the

best were splendid, not merely loud – persisted all through the century.

As well as the crowd-quelling voices of the actors the music was important in establishing mood and compelling a measure of attention – for music, as we all know, hath charms to soothe the savage breast. The orchestra was always in its place, lending excitement to scenes of mounting tension, supporting pathos when it was needed, and rousing the audience to patriotic fervour when that was appropriate. Nor was this music vulgar and coarse in its quality. Fine melodramas had accomplished musical scores, and rarely was a romantic play presented in which the actors were not required to sing, either singly or in harmonized pieces. The nineteenth-century actor was expected to be a singer, a dancer, a fencer, and an acrobat, able to perform feats of skill of the kind now achieved by 'stunt-men.' Edmund Kean, the greatest tragedian of the early part of the century, was also its finest Harlequin in his youth, when he had to do everything that was expected of an actor. These lion-voiced, acrobatic, musical players did not pay much attention to what is now called, by Method actors, 'the subtext'; they had to put across the primary text itself, and that was skilled, demanding work. It was a lively, bustling, highly coloured theatre, and in these qualities it mirrored the nature of its time.

This vivid, aggressive theatrical world could be

coarse in the hands of coarse performers, but capable of splendid achievement when the players were true artists. What was its audience?

In such a presentation as this I cannot go into detail about the rise and fall of the theatre audience as economic pressure or change of taste affected it. It must be enough to say that the audience at the beginning of the century was very large, that in the middle of the century the more refined part of it tended to prefer opera to drama, and that by the end of the century the audience was once again very large. But who were the people who were faithful to the theatre throughout? They were the poor, the more emancipated portion of the middle class, and people of artistic sensibility who, like the others, found in the theatre something without which they could not live completely.

What was that? It was the quality of fulfilment people seek in their amusements, and which may be found in dancing – which is physically delightful – or gambling – which provides an element of risk and even of danger in lives where it cannot otherwise be achieved – or music – an emotional taste, which always has its devotees – or the theatre, which is in part a literary taste. All of these pleasures satisfy deep instincts and drives, and bring the pleasure-seeker into touch with what is numinous, enlarging, emotionally and spiritually rich, in lives which may otherwise be overwhelmed by commonplaces. The theatre, which is our concern, meant freedom from the purely external world of job, of domesticity, and the pressing needs of everyday. It meant a world in which a pattern was imposed on the unmanageable stuff of life, and where justice might be seen at work in a society so often unjust. It meant a world in which the spectator – poor workingman and his female counterpart, or bourgeois citizen toiling to keep his place in a hurrying world – could equate himself with the Hero, the Heroine, or the Villain in a world of Myth, a world in which these archetypal figures worked out their destiny in an atmosphere where Poetic Justice, however tardy, would manifest itself after many trials and vicissitudes. It was a world of romance.

The theatre and its audience were very well aware of romance and what it meant. In terms of the nineteenth-century theatre that has never been more plainly stated than in the prologue Matthew Gregory Lewis wrote for his immensely popular drama, *The Castle Spectre*, which first appeared at Drury Lane Theatre in 1797. This is how it begins:

> *Far from the haunts of men, of vice the foe,*
> *The moon-struck child of genius and of woe,*
> *Versed in each magic spell, and dear to fame,*
> *A fair enchantress dwells, Romance her name.*
> *She loathes the sun or blazing taper's light:*
> *The moon-beam'd landscape and tempestuous night*

Alone she loves; and oft, with glimmering lamp,
Near graves new-open'd or midst dungeons damp
Drear forests, ruin'd aisles, and haunted towers,
Forlorn she roves, and raves away the hours!
Anon, when storms howl loud and lash the deep,
Desperate she climbs the sea-rock's beetling steep;
There wildly strikes her harp's fantastic strings,
Tells to the moon how grief her bosom wrings,
And while her strange song chaunts fictitious ills,
In wounded hearts Oblivion's balm distills.

That was, in broad terms, what the nineteenth century asked for when it went to the theatre – Oblivion's balm, a forgetfulness of the world of everyday. But we should be very far from the truth if we imagined these auditors – the upper-class Sir Mulberry Hawk and his friends, Pendennis and David Copperfield, sometimes Lord Byron and Sir Walter Scott; tallow-chandlers, lawyers' clerks, Charles Lamb's relatives, to speak of the middle-class; and all that extraordinary congeries of street-peddlers and coalheavers and dog-stealers and prostitutes and the whole world of low-life that we read of in Mayhew – as merely damp-eyed seekers for romance alone. Not a bit of it. In the slang of their own time, they knew perfectly well what o'clock it was, and that romance, though sweet on the palate, was not all there was to life.

Listen to the epilogue to that very same play,

which was spoken by one of the most popular co-
mediennes of the day, Mrs Jordan, who had played
the unhappy heroine Angela in *The Castle Spectre*.
She appeared afterward before the curtain to speak
the Epilogue, that sends the play up, in modern
parlance. Here is her summing up of the denoue-
ment:

> *All perforce, when I his crimes relate*
> *Must own that Osmond well deserved his fate,*
> *He heeded not papa's pathetic pleading;*
> *He stabbed mamma — which was extreme ill-breeding;*
> *And at his feet for mercy when I sued,*
> *The odious wretch, I vow, was downright rude,*
> *Twice his bold hands my person dared to touch!*
> *Twice in one day — 'Twas really once too much!*
> *And therefore justly filled with virtuous ire,*
> *To save my honour, and protect my sire,*
> *I drew my knife, and in his bosom stuckit*
> *He fell, you clapped, and then he kicked the bucket!*

And she concludes with a request to the audience
to make the play a great success, so that she may
stab her oppressor every night. The audience, having been happily led into a world of romance, is
returned to the world of comedy by a flirtatious
actress and an irreverent epilogue. The audience
did not mistake romance for reality, but it wanted
romance to sweeten reality.

Melodrama was not the only theatrical mode during the nineteenth century, but it was the dominant one. There were moves toward refinement of comedy, and they were successful. But most plays, including classical tragedies, partook of the melodramatic quality. The difference between the noble, classically spoken Hamlet of John Philip Kemble (1783) and the tempestuous Shylock of Edmund Kean in 1814 is the difference between Neo-Classicism and Romanticism; of Kemble it was said that he was 'the statue on the pedestal that cannot come down without shaming its worshippers'; we know that Coleridge said that watching Kean was like reading Shakespeare by flashes of lightning. Kemble might lift you to new heights of splendour, but Kean could make your flesh creep. It is interesting that some critics referred to Kean as a *radical* performer, and they meant it politically. Kean might have said, as another, very different, man said at the end of the century, that he had come to disturb the sleep of the world.

What is melodrama? Bernard Shaw defines it very justly in discussing the melodrama offered at the Adelphi Theatre during his time as a critic at the end of the century. He said: 'A really good Adelphi melodrama is very hard to get. It should be a simple and sincere drama of action and feeling, kept well within that vast tract of passion and motive which is common to the philosopher and the labourer, relieved by plenty of fun, and depending for variety of human character, not on the high comedy idiosyncracies which individualize people in spite of the closest similarity of age, sex and circumstances, but on broad contrasts between types of youth and age, sympathy and selfishness, the masculine and the feminine, the serious and the frivolous, the sublime and the ridiculous, and so on. The whole character of the piece must be allegorical, idealistic, full of generalizations and moral lessons. It must represent conduct as producing swiftly and certainly on the individual the results which in actual life it produces on the race in the course of many centuries.'

Shaw knew what he was talking about. He himself attempted a melodrama, *The Devil's Disciple* (1896), and found that he could not hit the right note; his concept was too intellectual, his humour too sharply honed, his view of life too individual. Not that intellectual content of the right sort is outside the world of melodrama. Shaw also says: 'A really good Adelphi melodrama is of first-rate literary importance, because it needs only elaboration to become a masterpiece' – and he instances several masterworks of European theatre which have the unmistakable mark of melodrama on them.

The principle of melodrama is enantiodromia, an impressive Greek word for a simple and familiar thing, sometimes called Poetic Justice. The Greek

word reminds us that the principle is of great antiquity; it was first enunciated by Heraclitus in the
fifth century BC. All extremes, said he, tend to run
into their opposites. This has been called the reg-
ulating function of antithesis. In common life, in
drama, and in fiction, we know it as the way in which
at last villains meet their downfall, the oppressed
are given their due, and compensating factors are
to be discerned in almost any human situation. The
principle appears in ordinary speech in such
expressions as 'It's always darkest before the dawn,'
and, more colloquially, 'Time wounds all heels.'

This is none the less a great principle of human
life because, sometimes in the cheapest melodrama,
life is narrowly and meanly conceived. 'Vengeance
is mine; I will repay, saith the Lord.' But in melodrama somebody, usually the hero, is made the in-
strument of the Lord's will, and we see him
triumphing over his adversaries, with right de-
monstrably on his side.

This is one of the most satisfying effects art can
produce, and we see it in works of exquisite subtlety
as well as in the roughest hack-work. Unhappily, it
is to the hack-work alone that most people apply
the term melodrama. They will not see the same
Heraclitean dictum at work in art they respect. But
it is the ground and strength of much, good and
bad, that is done on the stage. Truth, even when it

is absurdly propounded, is truth nonetheless, and enantiodromia is the understructure of a mighty truth.

During the nineteenth century no unmistakable dramatic masterpieces were written in the melodramatic mode until the coming of Ibsen, who learned so much of his stagecraft from those melodramatic experts Scribe and Sardou. By Ibsen's time the psychological climate of the literary world everywhere was creeping near to the mode of thinking which found its explication in the psychoanalysis of Sigmund Freud. The Romantic concern with the particularities of individual personality reached its logical peak in the thought of Freud; it was his one-time associate, Carl Gustav Jung, who opened up the Freudian world until it once again had space for the mythological and numinous background of European and American thought.

You may be surprised and perhaps affronted that I should link melodrama, Ibsen, and Freud in a single paragraph, but I hope that as these lectures continue I shall make my case for doing so. Freud did not spring full-blown into a world that had had no warning of his coming. Many of the insights he put in the form of scientific papers had already been hinted at by other medical scientists who had not wished to carry them through to general conclusions. Psychology and literature are never far apart, and many works of greater or lesser significance during the nineteenth century made it clear that what Freud had encountered in the consulting-room, writers had observed and understood intuitively in their work; Henry James and Henrik Ibsen are but two names far down on a list which counts Byron, Stendahl, Balzac, and Flaubert among its numbers.

Freud's great work on the interpretation of dreams appeared in 1900 and caused a slowly mounting uproar. But Ibsen had been causing his own uproar for at least twenty years before that, because his concern with human personality had led him inevitably to an investigation of the underside of what personality involved. In *A Doll's House* (1879), *Ghosts* (1881), *The Wild Duck* (1884), *Rosmersholm* (1886), *The Lady from the Sea* (1888), and other works whose names will occur to you, Ibsen holds the mirror up to nature in a way that many people could not endure, and his insights are Freudian, or perhaps we should say pre-Freudian. So far as we know, Ibsen never heard of Sigmund Freud. As Max Beerbohm says, it was one of the strengths of his strange, crustacean genius that he had never heard of anybody. But Freud knew about Ibsen, as those who have read his work in detail are well aware. This was the direction in which the nineteenth-century preoccupation with Romanticism led with an unsparing inevitability. What had been sweet in part changed to what people with a sweet tooth found intolerably bitter. But it was romance still. Did not Goethe say,

'Klassisch ist das Gesunde, Romantisch das Kranke' – Classicism is healthy, and Romanticism sickness, or, if you prefer it, the Classic possesses equilibrium and the Romantic suffers interruption of equilibrium. But I think we all know that some illnesses are necessary and salutary, and indeed should not be called sicknesses but processes of evolution. Oblivion's balm had become a burning cautery.

Has this a bearing on the early nineteenth-century melodrama of which I have been speaking? Yes, it has. Critics and historians of literature have explored the beginnings of Romantic drama with Goethe and Schiller, and have said much about its appearance in the works of Byron, while making the usual perfunctory judgement that Byron was not a successful playwright and had no wish to be one. I beg leave to doubt both statements. After his death several of Byron's plays achieved a certain popularity on the stage, in hacked-about forms that would not have pleased their author. But they had enough dramatic vitality to make them worthy of the attention of actors and managers who sought to please the public and to keep themselves solvent. If we had lived in Toronto between 1830 and 1850 we should have had opportunities to see several of Byron's plays on the stage, and as they were welcomed we must assume that they were adequately, if not opulently, acted and mounted. (It is a mistake, by the way, to think that Toronto was a theatrical wilderness in the early years of its history; it saw most of what was popular in London and New York within a year or two of its presentation in the larger cities.)

Byron's plays are certainly melodramas, and one of them, though it had the least stage success, offers melodrama of a high order. That is *Manfred* (1817), in which the Satanic hero is burdened with remorse because he has loved passionately and by so doing destroyed the woman he loved because she was his sister. He resorts to magic, descends to the underworld, demands to see the spirit of his lost love, and begs her forgiveness; but it is not forthcoming. He dies, reconciled to some sort of retribution in the afterworld for his crime. I will not be so bold as to say that it is impossible for the stage; certainly as a radio drama, accompanied by the music which was written for it by Robert Schumann, it has revealed poetic and dramatic splendour. If film ever rises to poetry of speech, as well as poetry of image, *Manfred* might make a fine film. Byron's day as a dramatist may be yet to come.

There were good reasons, of course, why Byron and the other great poets of his era – Shelley, Wordsworth, Keats, and the too greatly neglected Thomas Lovell Beddoes – either failed as dramatists or never reached the test. The theatre was not a place to attract a poet. Actors might be ignorant and coarse — we recall Browning's complaint that when Macready produced his *Strafford* Macready was the only one who knew what 'arraignment' meant or who Strafford was. The financial rewards were so trivial that only hacks or men wholly beglamoured by the stage could put up with them. But Byron's powerful influence was not exerted directly; in plays like *Mazeppa* (1831) by Milner, and *The Vampyre* by Planché (1820), we find Byronic romance and Byron's Fated Man in forms that the theatre, and the public, could encompass and admire.

In Byron's poem, which rings so much like Walter Scott, the hero of *Mazeppa* is the Polish youth whose love for his commander's wife is punished when he is strapped to the back of a wild horse and driven off to roam the plains of the Ukraine until at last the horse falls dead and he is rescued. The play is the work of an industrious hack named H.M. Milner, and in his version the heroine is not a wife, but a daughter, thereby excusing Mazeppa of any adulterous motive. The hero, unquestionably, is the horse, splendidly trained for its role by Ducrow, the great horse-trainer of his time. The horse does not die, as in the poem, but recovers from its adventure, as does Mazeppa himself, who rides the great horse at the head of an avenging army, to show the tyrant who is who, and perhaps also something about the radical and romantic spirit of horses.

The play was presented at Astley's, a very nine-teenth-century institution, in which the pit could be cleared of seats and used as a circus ring and an auxiliary to the presentation on the stage proper. Thus *Mazeppa* was presented with facilities for showing the wild ride which included a treadmill upon which the horse ramped and galloped, behind which a moving panorama, unfolded on rollers, displayed first the plains and then the banks of the Dneiper; stage wolves, howling, foaming, and snapping, pursued the horse from time to time, and overhead flapped an ingenious mechanical raven ready to swoop if Mazeppa or the horse yielded up the ghost. Up ramps and down ramps, over cataracts and knee-deep in real water plunged the splendid beast, until at last it left the stage and raced round and round the central ring. The audience, we know, was purged with pity and terror. Real terror, for here was no film, no stunt-man, but a real actor and a real horse, and accidents were always possible. No wonder, when the tyrant was at last made to yield in the circus ring, there were cheers for both player and horse.

This was not precisely Byron, but it was nearer Byron than one might expect in a popular theatre, offered to a predominantly working-class audience. *Mazeppa* has become, you see, a drama in which love conquers all, and the world of nature, as exemplified by the horse, is on the side of the right. This is Byron greatly coarsened, but it is Byronic still, and unquestionably it is romance.

In *The Vampyre* we meet the Byronic Fated Man, in this instance a Scottish earl named Ruthven, who is betrothed to Margaret, daughter of Ronald, the Baron of the Isles. Ronald does not know that his prospective son-in-law is a vampire, and on Ruthven's behalf it must be said that he is very sorry to deceive the father and drink the blood of the daughter, but he cannot resist his dreadful fate. It may be that he is not wholly displeased when, at the last moment, he is foiled, and having been struck by a thunderbolt, sinks into the earth.

Laugh a superior laugh if you will, but when next opportunity serves, look at a few episodes of *Dr Who* on television, and you will find that Ruthven is not as dead as might be supposed. Implacable evil is good drama, but evil plagued by scruple is better.

I cannot resist the pleasure of quoting to you Ruthven's soliloquy, which is one of my favourite gems of melodramatic rhetoric:

Demon as I am, that walk the earth to slaughter and devour! The little that remains of heart within this wizard frame, sustained alone by human blood, shrinks from the appalling act of planting misery in the bosom of this veteran chieftan. Still must the fearful sacrifice be made, and suddenly, for the approaching night will find my wretched

*frame exhausted – and darkness – worse than death –
annihilation is my lot! Margaret! unhappy maid! thou
art my destined prey! thy blood must feed a Vampire's life,
and prove the food of his disgusting banquet.*

Exploitation of the theme of the Fated Man took
countless forms and speculation about the popularity of this archetypal figure could engage us for
a long time, but two more examples must suffice.
One of these is *Vanderdecken*, the tale of the Flying
Dutchman, of which the earliest popular version
was written by Edward Fitzball in 1827. It was described to the public as a 'Nautical Burletta,' which
suggests something not too serious in treatment.
Certainly it contains a good deal of comedy and the
kind of high-spirited courage associated with sailors, but the figure of the Dutchman himself is sombre
and, since it was played by that powerful actor T.P.
Cook, it must have been thrilling. The legend is
well-known: A Dutch sea captain who has blas-
phemed against God during a storm is condemned
to roam the seas forever unless he can find a pure
woman whose unselfish love will redeem him; he
does find her, but she perishes with him. Modern
audiences are familiar with the theme as used by
Wagner in his splendid opera; it is interesting that
Wagner seems to have been influenced, in some
degree, by Fitzball's play. As we watch the opera
we cannot help but be aware that we are watching

nineteenth-century melodrama as animated by a genius, and in the course of these lectures I want to emphasize the fact that some of the best of the nineteenth-century theatre is still drawing capacity audiences wherever opera is enjoyed. If you think that fine music can redeem dramatic rubbish I disagree; my view is that the great composers of opera were also great men of the theatre and knew a first-rate theme, and a dramatic mode wholly friendly to music, when they saw it. They had the power to illuminate themes which were theatrically effective but not impressive as literature when they were given utterance by hacks like Fitzball and Milner.

I call your attention to the fact that in this popular thriller the Flying Dutchman hardly speaks at all. Indeed, he is under an injunction not to speak, or his suit to the pure-hearted heroine Lestelle will fail. But at last, under great dramatic pressure, he does speak, and in consequence, although he and Lestelle are united, it is not in this world.

Vanderdecken is almost speechless. The Monster in the very popular dramatization of *Frankenstein* by Milner does not speak at all. Mary Shelley wrote her tale of horror in 1818, and the dramatized version appeared in 1823, the unfortunate Monster being played by the most popular actor of monstrous roles of his time, Obi Smith. Those of you who know the original novel must have been impressed by the style of heightened but evocative and dignified narration in which it is cast. It has claims to be regarded as a philosophical novel, for the Monster created by Frankenstein is moved at first by noble and philanthropic feelings. He is disillusioned. He says: 'I learned that the possessions most esteemed by your fellow creatures were high and unsullied descent united with riches.' The inhumanity and cruelty of mankind corrupts him and he becomes a killer and most be hunted down – though he does not die, but escapes. This theme is maintained in the play, though the action undergoes compression, and romanticising, and it must also be said vulgarization, and at last, after having stabbed his creator, the monster dies by flinging himself into the crater of Mount Etna. A naked power and, it may also be said, a splendour is to be found in this crude play which is greater than anything I have encountered in the numerous moving pictures that have been made on the same theme. The reason, I think, is that films, even on fantastic themes, are held to the realism inherent in photography and they avoid elevated speech, not to speak of poetry. The theatre is not so bound and it may be that the true drama of Frankenstein and his fearsome creation is yet to reach the stage. The silence of the Monster is terrible even to the reader, and although Milner was a commonplace journeyman of the theatre we must credit him with the perception that silence can be, in some circumstances, horrifying as the most skilled rhetoric cannot. We pity the Monster because amid all those wagging tongues he alone has no speech, and this gives him a grotesque nobility.

Before we conclude today's exploration of this aspect of the drama of the nineteenth century, something should be said about the formula which underlies these plays, and scores of others like them. It is the structure of mingled plot, which has always been characteristic of the best plays written in English on either side of the Atlantic. It is a puzzle to many Continental critics, who cannot accept the notion that tragic or serious action may be interspersed with comedy, and even buffoonery. Do not ask me why English-speaking audiences not only love such a mingling, but insist upon it. Shakespeare was devoted to this principle, and we do not have to be profound critics to see that in his plays and in those of countless lesser dramatists the introduction of some comic action not only gives the audience a respite from the intensity of tragic or painful matters, but also provides assurance that tragedy is not all-encompassing. When Hamlet encounters the Gravediggers we are made aware that whatever of nature is mirrored in the intrigues in the Castle of Elsinore, here, in the open air, are people untouched by such considerations, people cheerful, wrong-headed, and yet possessed of a serenity of their own which is a sharp contrast to that aspect of nature which is leading inexorably to the slaughter that follows the duel between Hamlet and Laertes. The comedy is a balancing factor, a restorer of equilibrium, and a deeply serious principle of dramaturgy.

In melodrama the fortunes of the Hero and Heroine whose affairs are the main business of the play are partnered by two beings whom we had better call the Comic Man and the Comic Woman. They are either of social position inferior to the two principals, or they are unquestionably of another and far less serious order of being. They too have a love affair, but it is conducted on comic principles; the Comic Man may be extremely vain, or very greedy or invincibly stupid, and the Comic Woman treats him with appropriate scorn or merriment. They both have hearts of gold and push the action along often by the foolish mistakes they make. In a crisis they always turn up trumps, and not infrequently they give the Villain a piece of their minds in just such direct terms as the members of the audience would like to do.

Although of course I did not realize it at the time, I had the immense good fortune as a boy to go to the theatre in a town where the greater part of the audience was not illiterate in the sense that it was innocent of paper and ink – though even this was so in some instances – but was untouched by sophisticated notions of conduct or probability. In those days there were plenty of plays directed at just such people, and plenty of actors who knew nothing of subtext, but knew plenty about holding the attention and engaging the loyalty or the hatred of the spectators. So, late in the day, but not too late, I saw something of how plays built on this principle worked, and I was enough of a critic even then to recognize that the Comic Man was often the most accomplished actor on the stage.

In *Uncle Tom's Cabin* (1852), when we were so-bered, and sometimes tearful, because of the hard-ships of the slaves, how heart-warming it was when Marks the Lawyer appeared, very drunk and mounted unsteadily on the back of a donkey. When the moral splendour of Little Eva St Clair was be-coming almost too much for our powers of admi-ration, how we applauded Topsy, who turned cart-wheels and leered invitingly at us every time she delivered a funny line; we were flattered that she took us into her confidence in this way, for the stupid people on the stage never seemed to see the joke, and we shared it with her. So thus I sat, in the twenties of this century, unaware of the fact that I was not far away from the audience in the Cobourg or Astley's a century before. There is something to be said for provincialism and time-lag, after all.

I even saw, as a portion of a minstrel show, a version of the Faust legend that bore about the same relationship to Goethe's mighty drama that a crushed cabbage-leaf in a market gutter bears to the gardens of Versailles. But when the Devil appeared in a puff of smoke, roaring 'Fear me not, good people, for I will not harm ye!', the greater part of the audience shrank in alarm. It was a religious town, you see, and we all knew that the Devil was very near.

It was crude, it was coarse, but it was very effective. Let us not forget that nowadays everybody sees the best that film and television have to offer – such as that is – and what is seen in New York and London is also seen in just such towns as the one of which I have been speaking. There has been an extraordinary development of sophistication among audiences, and a corresponding increase in their expectations. Our theatrical culture is unified and blenderized. But there are undying elements in melodrama, and as I have already said, and will say again, we know this if we are opera-goers. We know it if we are perceptive viewers of film or television.

Today I have spoken about melodrama in general terms, and as oblivion's balm. Tomorrow I shall talk about women in melodrama, and shall attempt to trace the development of the general concept of what a woman is, and what her experience in life may be, that took place during the nineteenth century. The revolt that finds modern expression in Women's Lib began at least 182 years ago, and it is clear for us to trace, in the history of the parts women played on the stage, how men saw them, and how they saw themselves.

The title of that lecture, for reasons that I shall hope to make plain, is 'The Lost Lady.'

LECTURE TWO

❧

The Lost Lady

SINCE ACTRESSES TOOK, and held, their place on the English-speaking stage in 1660, there has been no lack of plays written to throw a female character into prominence and often into the leading position in the drama. The theatre of the nineteenth century was truly a mirror of the nature of the society it served in the attention it paid to women, and the position it accorded to a succession of actresses of great abilities.

Obviously it saw women in nineteenth-century terms. Every age has its idea of what women are, just as it has its idea of what men may be. When I was preparing these lectures I warned myself sternly to keep clear of generalities, but, like cheerfulness, they will keep breaking in. I think it may be said that in any age men and women of exceptional qualities may be anything they choose, if they have the power of personality or intellect, or spirit, to get away with it. Every great actor or actress compels the public to accept him or her as an interpretative agent who is, in a very real sense, an artefact. It is the blazing Edmund Kean we remember as glorious, rather than his intellectual, scholarly son

Charles; it is Henry Irving – who appears to have
been like nothing in the heavens above or in the
earth beneath, or in the waters under the earth –
who dominated the stage for twenty-five years and
forced the phlegmatic English to accept acting as
one of the arts. Among actresses it is Sarah Siddons,
who was so sodden with tragedy that she spoke
blank verse in private life, and Ellen Terry, who
could charm a bird out of a tree even when she was
physically unsuited to the roles of young girls, and
Sarah Bernhardt, whose attraction had about it a
strong whiff of brimstone, and Eleanora Duse, who
could blush so that you saw the blood mounting
above her bosom like wine mounting in a jug, who
made the theatre a temple, when intellectual Fabian
ladies like Janet Achurch were in despair because
they could not turn it into a lecture hall. It was
because the great players, men and women, were
extraordinary people that they could compel their
audiences to accept plays that are not, in themselves,
remarkable.

For years I have been telling my students that the
theatre is a coarse art. By that I mean that it is coarse
as music is coarse; it appeals immediately to primary, not secondary elements in human nature,
and if drama and music cannot grab you with a fine
strong effect, all the elaboration of intellectual art
will go for nothing. Drama and music must appeal
to people who are not learned in critical theory as

well as to the highly informed; the primary assault must be upon the senses, not upon the intellect. Once the emotional pressure has been achieved, refinements of all kinds, and of the uttermost tenuity, are possible, but they are not in themselves capable of creating and sustaining great art. Refinement must be made upon heavy ore, not upon cobwebs.

In the nineteenth century women on the stage had to be presented in terms that women and men in the audience would accept and, the more we look at nineteenth-century theatre repertoire, the more we understand how wide that range of acceptance was.

It included every sort of woman who has been identified by one of the foremost female psychologists of our time, Irene Clarement de Castillejo. One is the Mate and Mother, and her opposite, the Witch or Destructive Woman. Another is the Hetaera or Companion, whose negative aspect is the Harlot. Third is the Amazon, and her shadow aspect is the Termagant or Brawling Woman. Fourth, and rarest, is the Medium, the woman in touch, it seems, with things not normally accessible, and her negative aspect is the Madwoman, always more terrifying to men than to her own sex. They all appeared on the nineteenth-century stage, time and again.

For several decades of this century it was popularly believed that the women of the nineteenth century conformed to, and were forced into the mould of, the Mate-Mother figure. This is the submissive, but quietly wise, woman, who makes the home and cares for the children while her man goes into the world and has adventures, or at least brings home the livelihood. But women of character are rarely confined to a single female role, as de Castillejo makes very clear, and as we know if we pay attention to nineteenth-century biographies and memoirs. A clever woman could play the Mother-Mate role with one hand tied behind her, and have plenty of energy left to be a Hetaira to her husband and perhaps a number of other men, without necessarily falling into the negative side of the character and becoming a Whore. She could also play the Amazon, and frequently did so, for among privileged women hunting, travel, and exploration were favourite pastimes; there are indications that the negative side of this type, the Termagant, or Brawler, was not unknown. And there were women of strongly spiritual and intuitive character, who now and then became Madwomen.

It is not our task here to pursue this typology very far, but a few familiar figures will illustrate its applicability in the nineteenth century. Anthony Trollope's wife was unquestionably a wise and companionable Mate to a man who needed one badly, and Bulwer-Lytton's wife was beyond doubt the destructive Witch in the life of her husband. (She even screamed his shortcomings at him from the Ladies' Gallery of the House of Commons.) The Baroness Burdett-Coutts was a distinguished Hetaera and patron to many men of talent, as was Ellen Terry. Of Whores I forbear to speak at length, though perhaps the notorious Lady Caroline Lamb may be mentioned in passing. The county-gentry provided numberless Amazons, fox-hunting women of whom Lady Gay Spanker, in Boucicault's Comedy *London Assurance* (1841), offers us an attractive picture; and Isabel Burton as an explorer, and Florence Nightingale, terror of governmental departments, are further examples. Of Termagants it is also perhaps wiser to offer a figure in literature, and I suggest the aggrieved and uproarious Mrs Caudle, in Douglas Jerrold's *Mrs Caudle's Curtain Lectures* (1845), a book thought very funny by several generations, but which now makes painful reading. As the Medium, I suggest Elizabeth Barrett-Browning, and as the Madwoman, Thackeray's unhappy wife, who was confined for many years but never ceased to be a dominating figure in the mind and affairs of her husband. There are, of course, women who contrive to play at various times all these roles, and a case could be made for Queen Victoria herself as a portmanteau exemplar, for what Shakespeare says about one man in his time playing many parts is equally true of women.

Only in the simplest drama are women shown as

embodiments of one type, but there was much simple drama and there is a psychological reason for this extreme attitude. In a society where women live under substantial political and economic restraints – and the nineteenth century was unquestionably such an age – men of simple psychology are apt to assert a form of chattel-right in the women – usually the wife or the beloved – who are foremost in their lives. This is only partly an economic attitude; it goes deeper than money and land. The woman is regarded as an extension of the man's total being, and sometimes she is referred to by psychologists as the External Image of his Soul, or perhaps the Vessel of his Honour. This attitude goes at least as far back as the Age of Chivalry, and in ideal conditions it could encourage knightly conduct toward women and a regard for them which is psychologically extreme, and can be sustained only if both parties to the relationship agree to play it as a game. Bernard Shaw has satirized such a relationship acutely in *Arms and the Man,* in which the vainglorious soldier Sergius Saranoff and his ideal love, Raina Petkoff, play this game to a point of splendid absurdity, until it is exploded by the matter-of-fact Swiss soldier Bluntschli, who regards Raina as a woman – idealized certainly, but at least a human being, and not a Romantic abstraction.

Much of the disillusion in marriage, of which so many nineteenth-century writers make a great deal, is rooted in the unreality of this sort of relationship which was maintained in the face of facts for a very long time and is by no means dead yet. I hope you will not think me cynical if I say that other unrealities are supplanting this one in our own day, of which the ideal of perfect liberty in sexual relationships is one.

Idealized women are not common in the comedy of the eighteenth century, but, as I said yesterday, the dawn of the Romantic era at the beginning of the nineteenth century made them as thick as blackberries. A fine comedy of the year 1800, Thos. Morton's *Speed The Plough*, offers an example. The heroine is a farmer's daughter, Susan Ashfield, and you can spot her as the heroine the moment she comes on the stage, saying 'My dear home, thrice welcome!', for she speaks in an elegant style quite unlike that of her parents, Farmer and Dame Ashfield. This is important, for in melodrama of the purest sort heroes and heroines are splendid speakers, positive Roman candles of simile and metaphor. W.S. Gilbert, who wrote melodrama and could also satirize it shrewdly, gives us an exaggerated, but not greatly exaggerated, example of this hero-and-heroine eloquence in *H.M.S. Pinafore*, in which Ralph Rackstraw, the simple foremast hand, is declaring his love for his Captain's daughter. She calls him by name, to which he replies:

Aye, lady, no other than poor Ralph Rackstraw.

Josephine is overcome:

How my heart beats!

she says, and then, aloud:

And why poor, Ralph?

Whereupon the simple seaman, the butt of epau-letted scorn, the mark of quarterdeck derision, re-plies:

I am poor in the essence of happiness, lady – rich only in never-ending unrest. In me there meet a combination of antithetical elements which are at eternal war with one another. Driven hither by objective influences – thither by subjective emotions – wafted one moment into blazing day, by mocking hope – plunged the next into the Cimmerian darkness of tangible despair, I am but a living ganglion of irreconcilable antagonisms. I hope I make myself clear, lady?

And Josephine says, aside:

His simple eloquence goes to my heart!

This is satire, but it is a satire that reveals truth

better than a dozen direct quotations from melodrama. If you wish to pursue a study of melodrama
by an easy path, you will find much of what was
absurd about it in Gilbert's libretti for *The Pirates of
Penzance*, *Pinafore*, and *Ruddigore*. But you will not
find the whole truth about it in Gilbert, by any means.

As I hope I have already established, the hero
and heroine of melodrama were idealized versions
of the simple people in their audience, and simple
people did not like simple speech; they wanted to
be magniloquent, even if by proxy.

Their women were allowed to speak splendidly
and sometimes movingly, but they were not allowed
to do much. In the popular drama *The Miller and
His Men* (1813), which held the stage for more than
fifty years, the heroine Claudine is not even given
much to say; she is imperilled and rescued, but
between her father and her lover she hardly dares
to open her mouth except in their commendation.
It is the bandit's mistress Ravina who has the good
lines that are allotted to women, and it is Ravina
who, in the spectacular conclusion, blows up the
mill.

So also in *Black Eyed Susan* the heroine supplies
the title, but her function in the play is to display
from time to time the kind of purity for which Sweet
William is ready to endanger his life. When that
purity is threatened she can say: 'Sir, scorn has no
word – contempt no voice to speak my loathing of

your insinuations. Take, sir, all that is here; satisfy your avarice – but dare not indulge your malice at the cost of one who has now nothing left in her misery but the sweet consciousness of virtue.'

The faithful, pure wives are numberless, but the faithful, pure daughters run them a close second. The nineteenth century is supposed to have made a fetish of motherhood, but on the stage fathers demanded at least equal and sometimes superior rights. Such fathers usually have no wives, so their honour and their external soul is exemplified by their daughters, such as Virginia, in the tragedy of *Virginius* (1820) whose father kills her rather than behold her dishonour; in Bulwer's *Richelieu* (1839) his ward, Julie de Mortemar, is so precious that when the King wants her for his vile purposes, the great Cardinal invokes the whole might of Mother Church to defend her; in *The Corsican Brothers* (1852) the honour of Julie de Lesparre is the occasion of two duels and two deaths. In *Olivia* (1885), a dramatization of *The Vicar of Wakefield*, the heroine has something to say for herself, but it is her father who seems to feel her dishonour most deeply. These heroines were all great sufferers, and their extreme seriousness of mind makes us wonder if, in less intense situations, they might not have been rather heavy company. There is no hint of the Hetaera about any of them. But of course there have always been men who have never considered a friendly relationship with a woman, and such men are by no means confined to the least educated or least privileged class.

Were there no jolly girls and no intelligent girls, then, in the drama of the nineteenth-century? Indeed there were, but in the melodramas they appear as secondary characters, or Comic Women. In comedy they made frequent appearance, though here it was not uncommon for the girls to be simply good conduct prizes, to be claimed at the end of the play by the adventurous, witty boys. We find them, for example in *Our Boys* (1875) and in a late play for our period, *Charley's Aunt* (1892), to name but two which ran for well over 1300 performances at their initial production.

Intelligent and witty women were not uncommon among comedy heroines. But for the most lively sort of amusing women we have to look at a category of entertainment which is little seen on our stage today, but which was continuously popular in the last century. I mean satirical and burlesque plays.

If a drama made a hit in the nineteenth century, it was not long before a burlesque version of it appeared in a popular theatre. There must have been a large group of playgoers who were so well acquainted with what was on the serious stage that they were able to appreciate genial and often subtle burlesque versions on the lighter stage. The existence of serious drama and burlesque versions of it is conclusive evidence that the nineteenth century, as a whole, was in no doubt about the nature of theatrical illusion. Apparently people who enjoyed melodrama also provided the audience for melodramatic spoofs like *The Rosebud of Stinging Nettle Farm* (1862). If you did not know one you could not appreciate the other. This was an instance of enantiodromia: the heavily weighted moral drama ran into a farcical anti-masque, a burlesque of itself.

The study of nineteenth-century burlesque is of the greatest psychological interest, for much of its attraction lay in its transvestite element. The leading comedian played a female role, and the hero was represented by a pretty girl with a striking stage personality and excellent legs. A great mimic who specialized in this sort of thing was Fred Leslie, and on more than one occasion the Lord Chamberlain had to remind him that offensive caricature of living persons was not to be encouraged. He caricatured Gladstone; he caricatured Henry Irving. Reputedly he was very funny, and the kind of people who delight in derision and jeering at the famous were delighted and, as this is a very numerous group of the total population, Leslie was something of a public scourge. What made his burlesque particularly disagreeable to his victims was that he did it while ridiculously got up in women's clothes. But any of his female counterparts who had a talent for mimicry might caricature any number of men, and nobody minded. Why, one wonders? Perhaps it was because Leslie was grotesque and the women were not; they were professionally charming. Irving did not mind being imitated by Cissie Loftus.

Actresses of this sort had to be talented as well as beautiful; they were expected to sing and dance, and never to fail in their enchantment. A particular favourite of mine in this group is Louisa Fairbrother, who was born in 1816, and very early specialized in men's roles in light entertainment. There are portraits of her, as Little John in *Robin Hood* (1846), and Eglantine in *Valentine and Orson* (1844), and in *Ali Baba* (1850); she frequently wore a piquant moustache and tiny beard, and if we may believe her portraits she was what would then have been described as a stunner. Her fate is interesting; in 1840, when she was 24, she was morganatically married to the Duke of Cambridge, who was 21, but she did not for that reason leave the stage. She retired in her own good time. Did she come to an unhappy end? Not she! She lived in great style in Queen Street, Mayfair, until her death in 1890, where she was recognized as a figure of unimpeachable respectability, known as Mrs Fitzgeorge.

My point is that lachrymose heroines were not the only female roles available on the nineteenth-century stage. Charm, a lively spirit, and beauty were accorded their usual due. We may ask ourselves why it was particularly pleasing to see a handsome young woman assuming masculine attributes and a version of masculine manners, while retaining all her feminine charm. Why was this linked with a very strong and sometimes fierce kind of comedy, provided by a man dressed as a grotesque caricature of a woman? This kind of fun was immensely popular, especially in Christmas pantomime, at least until 1914, and it persisted in a limited form for twenty years after that. If we pursue this question we may find ourselves becoming very solemn about the satyr plays of Ancient Greece, or the Atellan Comedies of Ancient Rome, or the rough farces of the Middle Ages and the pre-Shakespearean comedy, in which, of course, roles like Gammer Gurton and her gossip Dame Catte were played by men. But no such display of historical knowledge throws any light on the girls of the nineteenth century who became popular favourites by plastering a caricature of manliness over their female charm.

Here we are in danger of becoming humourlessly and imperceptively psychological in our search for explanations. Surely it is enough to say that these girls gave a display of skill, piquantly spiced with a kind of sexual attraction to which most men are susceptible, and which is neither masculine nor feminine, but androgynous. These jolly stars of burlesque are of the family of Rosalind and Viola – of the boy actors of the earlier English stage. The her-

maphrodite, though a freak in nature, is psychologically a representation of completeness, of unity.

But now, having made my small psychological
point, what is there to say about the men who played
women as screaming viragos and anarchic mockers
of the pillars of society? Surely they, too, stand in
a line that is of great antiquity? In the spring of
1982 London audiences flocked to Drury Lane to
watch Barry Humphries, an Australian comedian,
who dresses himself as Edna Everidge, and makes
wild fun of the middle-class, middlebrow woman.
I have seen him, and as well as being very funny,
there is a savagery about his satire which is both
thrilling and alarming. He shows us womanhood
on the rampage; he shows us the maenad-figure,
not as a young woman possessed by a god, but as
a middle-aged woman possessed by ramping, roaring, monstrous egotism. And as both sexes appear
to admire him equally, we must assume that he tells
us something about our society which we suspect,
but dare only acknowledge when we are in the theatre, which, daubed and spattered as it is by com-
mercialism on the one hand and a foolish
intellectualism on the other, is still a temple of the
emotions and intuitions. There is a No Man's Land,
and No Woman's Land, between the sexes which
yields very special aspects of comedy.

As the nineteenth century wore on, the frank

melodrama of which we have been speaking was joined by another kind of melodrama, superficially less violent in its assaults on the emotions, but powerful because it presented an idealized picture of domestic life, and frequently of rural life.

There will be those among you who have seen late film versions of these popular favourites, some of which held the stage for thirty years and more. They were very common on the American stage, but they transplanted readily to England. One was *The Old Homestead* (1887) which is not a play in any strict sense, but an entertainment devised by a vaudeville actor, Denman Thompson, in which, as Josiah Whitcomb, he appeared as the proprietor of a farm where very little agricultural work was done, but where there was lots of squaredancing, Bible-quoting, low comedy, and homely wisdom; it counted among its agricultural workers a male quartet which, without any particular dramatic reason, obliged with closely harmonized versions of such ditties as 'The Old Oaken Bucket' and 'All Bound 'Round with A Woollen String.' But there is a theme: Josh's darling son has strayed to the Big City and been corrupted, and Josh, by sheer goodness of heart, wins him back to the true values of life.

I would not refer to this piece if it did not exemplify in a gross form a belief which has its roots in Romanticism, and might even have been approved by Wordsworth, though Byron would have been torn between scorn and laughter. That belief is simply that the truest morality inheres in rural life, which is represented as untainted by cynicism, opportunism, and moral looseness. This is, of course, quite untrue, and novelists and playwrights of this century have demonstrated its untruth in, for instance, the novels of William Faulkner, and such plays as *Tobacco Road*. The idealized Rousseauesque peasantry presented by poets of the earlier part of the nineteenth century have become the idealized rural middle class of its later years. As we look at Josiah Whitcomb now, we may perhaps think him a sanctimonious know-all, a social embarrassment, and tedious to a degree that makes Polonius seem a delightful companion. His most tiresome characteristic is perhaps his assertion of an ignorant rusticity as superior to a more enlightened kind of life, which he inevitably regards as wholly false, with its concern with good food, dirty French novels, and what he of course calls op'ry.

Josh and his innumerable brothers and sisters were very popular on the nineteenth-century stage, and I suppose they aroused in audiences that regret for lost innocence which is a strong psychological factor in societies marked by upward mobility. As you sip your expensive whisky you yearn, or think you yearn, for the days when you drank buttermilk.

The gravest and most disillusioning punishment that could be devised for people so affected would be to send them back to the farm.

Josh Whitcomb had lost his son to the fleshpots. But that was not the gravest loss possible on the Old Homestead, or at the Old Mill – for an astonishing number of melodramatic characters lived in mills. Our purpose is not to talk about economics, but in passing it may be said that many of these millers, monsters of industry though they were, seemed to be disastrous men of business. They were always signing papers they had not read, which later almost, but not quite, cost them the mill. Or they fell into debt, and were thus the prey of moneylenders and that fearful creature the Sheriff. The mortgage was epidemic, and bankers were men without bowels. By some chronological freak, mortgages tended to fall due on Christmas Eve. But these misfortunes paled before the greater misfortune of the Ruined Daughter. Millers' daughters had fatal attraction, and apparently no powers of resistance. They were also uncommonly fecund; afforded a single sexual encounter they were very soon moping and weeping and, as contemporary stage pictures inform us, took to wearing black shawls.

How did the Miller and his wife meet this not uncommon misfortune? With total unreason. A superior example of this sort of drama is *Hazel Kirke* (1880), a commonplace example is the immensely

popular *Way Down East* (1898). In *Hazel Kirke* the
seducer is not a seducer at all, but because he is a
nobleman it is assumed that he can be up to no
good when he declares that he loves Miller Kirke's
daughter. Old Kirke, apparently without any conception that there might be a faulty morality in his
action, has promised her hand to an elderly friend
who has lent him money to save the Mill. Here we
have the chattel concept of women clearly exemplified. The girl and her high-born lover elope, and
are married – a Scotch marriage at Gretna Green.
They live in high style, though the girl has the oblig-
atory regret for the Old Mill, and prompt to the
hour they have a Little Blessing. But then – Oh,
Horror! – it appears that they were married, not in
Scotland, but a few feet on the wrong side of the
Border, because the nobleman's Irish valet assumed
that the nobleman merely wished to have his will
with Hazel and then throw her aside, like a faded
flower.

The girl's agony is intense, but it is nothing to
the agony of her father, the Miller, who curses her,
goes blind, and is on the brink of losing the Mill.
(I should explain that the playwright, Steele McKaye,
wrote the part of the father for himself, so he naturally gets the lion's share of the agony.) But at last
the situation is resolved: it appears that the schem-
ing valet, being an Irishman, naturally made a mess
of his villainy, and the marriage *was* on the Scottish

side of the Border, with all that that implies in moral terms. Happiness! The Mill saved! Father and daughter reconciled.

It is astonishing to us, perhaps, that this was taken seriously by literally millions of playgoers. They were prepared to believe that the Miller was a fine old fellow, chock-a-block with moral nobility. They were prepared to believe that his daughter, who had been brought up by this monster in the morally warped atmosphere of the Mill, was just the wife for a young man in distinguished society. They were prepared to believe that the young man's mother, when she discovered that he was not married to Hazel, died of a stroke, presumably in order to sustain the family honour, and make the young couple feel cheap. But let us not be hard on those audiences. In our day we have believed some absurdities in the playhouse, too.

As for *Way Down East*, it is a simpler drama, and the heroine is brought near to death for her seeming transgression. Perhaps some of you have seen the old film in which Lilian Gish gives a good portrait of this submissive girl. Since the days of *Jane Shore*, plenty of people have believed that

> *When lovely woman stoops to folly,*
> *And finds too late that men betray,*
> *What charm can soothe her melancholy?*
> *What art can wash her tears away?*

The only art her guilt to cover,
To hide her shame from every eye,
To give repentance to her lover,
And wring his bosom is — to die.

And of course, in dying, she must be sure to take that embarrassing baby with her.

If we become widely acquainted with nineteenth-century drama we may be surprised by the fact that, while countless humble girls are considered suitable wives for young noblemen, we never meet with the converse, in which some virtuous farm lad marries a lady. The popular idea that love levels all ranks only works one way; this is the theme that Gilbert plays with so delightfully in *H.M.S. Pinafore.* If a woman of quality married beneath her, it was a subject for comedy, or more probably for not very delicate farce.

The explanation is that which I gave in the first of these lectures: the Heroine is the External Soul or the Vessel of Honour of the Hero, and therefore what matters most about her is her unspotted purity. The soul being, at least in the nineteenth century, conceived of as a feminine element, and virtue being a speciality of rural life, a girl like Hazel Kirke was acceptable, if not totally credible. Occasionally, in drama, we meet with a man who is wholly in the grip of conventional virtue; such a character is the young priest in Henry Arthur Jones' melodrama *Michael and His Lost Angel* (1896). The logical question is, Why should a man not be as sexually chaste as a woman? The answer seems to be that his area of honour and scruple, at least as exemplified in popular theatre, lies elsewhere, and for the continuity of the human race that may be just as well.

Have any of the plays and types of plays I have spoken of thus far anything to do with the revolution in social attitudes I spoke of yesterday, and which I called, for the sake of convenience, the Freudian Revolution? The answer is no; such plays as these were unthinkingly devoted to the accepted morality of their audiences. But there were other plays, seen at the same time, which we must now consider, that led directly toward radical changes in moral ideas, and the first of these is Kotzebue's *The Stranger* (1798), which was a translation of his drama of 1789 *Menschenhass und Reue*, which is translatable as *Misanthropy and Repentance*; it held the stage in Europe, England, and America for just about a century, which is a very long time for a play which is by no means of classic stature. Indeed, *The Stranger* is a bad play, full of over-strained rhetoric, pompous moralizing, and tears; too much is said and too little done, but at the heart of it there is a new idea, which is that marriages do not go astray because only one partner is at fault, and that a wife who has made a mistake deserves a hearing and a second chance.

The Stranger of the English title is Count Waldbourg, whose life has been embittered because his
friends proved false to him, and one of them in-
duced his young wife to elope. Waldbourg becomes
a misanthrope, reduced to a single servant, but not,
it appears, to any form of gainful employment. He
finds his secluded hovel on the estate of another
nobleman, in whose entourage is a woman, a Mrs
Haller, who is oppressed by a secret sorrow, and is
known far and wide for her charity to the poor and
her nobility of nature. She is, of course, the runaway
wife, whose seducer has deserted her. She and
Waldbourg are brought together by a high-minded
friend, who himself loves Mrs Haller unavailingly,
and at the end we see them reconciled by the appearance of their children, against whose claims to
a properly constituted family they are unable to
sustain, in the Count's case, his misanthropy, and
in Mrs Haller's case, her repentance, dear though
these emotional indulgences are. But as the story
unfolded we learned that the Count married his
wife when she was sixteen, neglected her because
he was so busy doing good, and thus paved the way
for her transgression. He forgives her, but we are
also led to believe that she forgives him, and they
are going to make a fresh start, having learned a
thing or two from their unhappiness.

This does not sound revolutionary now, but in
its clear statement that there may be two sides to
an infidelity it was something new. Within the last

two years the diaries of Cosima Wagner have been made available in translation, and I suggest that *The Stranger* is greatly illuminated by them. Cosima, the daughter of Franz Liszt, married the musician Franz von Bülow, who was not the most interesting of husbands for a woman who had grown up in a brilliant circle, and in the course of time she bolted with his friend and artistic hero, Richard Wagner. It was not easy to do, and as we read of her attempts to maintain some sort of reasonable relationship with von Bülow, and with those of her children who remained in his care, while serving the needs of the fiercely egotistical Wagner, we see what such a situation meant in nineteenth-century terms. Cosima was a woman of unusual intelligence, but she was a creature of her era, and she suffered in the mode of her era. Von Bülow behaved with exemplary dignity and good sense in a situation which was, in nineteenth-century terms, ignominious. These were three very serious people, not creatures of stage melodrama, but it was in the melodramatic mode of feeling that lay so heavily on the nineteenth century and which its theatre reflects, that they had to live out their destiny. The man or woman who can go directly against the spirit of his age is a person of the uttermost rarity; Byron attempted it and his partial success was bought at an inordinate price. The theatre seldom goes against the spirit of the age, for it is the mirror of nature. But it must yield to revolutions which occur outside its walls, as we shall see.

For a little while longer, however, we may profitably look at the spirit of the nineteenth century as it applied to women in theatrical terms. As you realize, these were special terms, not applicable to the novel or poetry, for those were enjoyed and understood in solitude, whereas theatre pleasure was a public pleasure, and what one saw in the playhouse – with the lights full on, remember – one was assumed in some measure to condone. Even to visit the playhouse committed one to an attitude. Lewis Carroll advised his readers to shun the playhouse unless they felt that, if stricken within its walls, they might blamelessly die there. (As Stanley Holloway was to say, in our own age, 'Don't die in a pub, it looks bad.') Think about what it means to visit a theatre with a consideration that you might die there, and you will have found out something about the nineteenth century.

In our times, death is somewhat hidden away. Not so with our ancestors, for whom it had horrors and satisfactions which are unknown to us.

> *Ah, lovely appearance of death!*
> *What sight upon earth is so fair?*
> *Not all the gay pageants that breathe*
> *Can with a dead body compare.*

So wrote Charles Wesley in his admired poem 'On

The Sight of a Corpse,' and the attitude was a familiar one for a century or more. Death is not Oblivion, but Penitence, Pardon, and Peace. For erring women in melodrama, Death settles all scores.

Consider the extremely popular melodrama which was concocted from Mrs Henry Wood's novel *East Lynne* (1863). The novel is by no means an unsophisticated piece of work; the play, however, is coarsely made, scenes of flat comedy being sandwiched between the sub-plot about an unjust accusation of murder, and the principal plot, which tells how Lady Isabel Vane married a worthy commoner, Archibald Carlyle, and was tempted from his home by the callous villain, Sir Francis Levison. Levison is overdrawn, but perhaps not so much as might be supposed. If we look at the first meeting between Tess of the Durbervilles and the villainous Alec Durberville, we find that his words to her are, 'Well, my Beauty, what can I do for you?' and he reflects, 'What a crummy girl' – crummy meaning, of course, of a confectionery-like deliciousness. We must assume that Victorian villains did to some extent talk like Levison. He has a child by Lady Isabel, but she refuses to marry him; the inconvenient child dies and she slinks back to East Lynne to care for her earlier child, Willy; she disguises herself as a governess, Madame Vine. She wears dark glasses, draws her hair back from her brow, and is thus impenetrably concealed from her former husband.

(All through its history the stage has chosen to ignore the fact that a really effective disguise is a matter of the uttermost difficulty.) Willy dies, and then Isabel dies, repentant, in the arms of her Archibald.

Isabel can only be described as a fool, and when we consider her eavesdropping, her unjust suspicions, and her total egotism we must say that she is an unpleasant fool. But I have had personal experience of this play, which I once directed with a company of very good actors; it was our intention to burlesque it, but we quickly discovered that its comic scenes needed no burlesque, and that its pathetic passages could only be burlesqued if one chose to stoop to a nasty sort of jeering. So we played it straight, and every night audiences were attentive, appreciative, and not infrequently tearful when first Little Willy died, and then Lady Isabel died. It was a peep into the past, and the past appeared strange, but not ridiculous. There was life in those seemingly dead bones.

The death of Willy sobered the audience because nobody of decent mind thinks the death of a child funny. The death of Little Eva St Clair in *Uncle Tom's Cabin* never failed for the same reason; lachrymose and sentimental though the lines may seem, there lies beneath them, and at the heart of the scene in which they occur, all that pathos of lost hope that the death of a child evokes. The Victorians, who knew of the death of children in a way we have happily forgotten, were moved even by a crude depiction of such a death.

So also with Lady Isabel. She may be a fool, and she may have made a mess of her life through her own doing, but, as Edgar Allen Poe has told us, the death of a beautiful young woman is a powerful poetic image, and we are moved by it, and by the repentance and renewed love that it brings about. As I have said before, the playwrights of the nineteenth century may have been wanting in literary skill, but they knew where to look for powerful and moving situations. Because our modern playwrights seem to be embarrassed by death, except the retributive deaths of criminals, we cannot assume that death has lost any of its pathos or its terror when we encounter it in the drama of the past.

A much more skilful play than *East Lynne*, that ends with the death of a foolish, vain, but pitiable woman, is *Froufrou* (1869), adapted from the French original of Henri Meilhac and Ludovic Halévy. Froufrou is the pet name of Gilberte Brigard, so called because that is the noise her beautiful silken dresses make when she moves. Froufrou is everybody's pet, but nobody takes her seriously, and so she does not take herself seriously, and gets into a complicated muddle. She so neglects her husband and child that her husband turns to her sister for what he expects of a wife, and Froufrou runs off with a seducer, whom her husband kills in a duel, which is sad because the seducer was not really a bad fellow. She too returns to her home in order to see the child she once neglected, and there she dies.

What did she and Lady Isabel die of? Of remorse, of swelling of the soul, of a sense that life has become unendurably complex – of an ailment which we might call Heroine's Disease. But Lady Isabel and Froufrou appealed to huge audiences of women who doubtless had, deep within them, a sense of having somehow been wronged, misunderstood, insufficiently loved – a sense that if they died people would understand how wonderful they had been.

We do not dismiss or diminish this emotion by calling it self-pity, for self-pity is a pervasive ailment, afflicting both men and women, and I do not see that it is, unless immoderately indulged, harmful or unjustified. Who knows our situation as we know it ourselves? Which of us can solemnly swear that he or she has never reflected in some low moment, 'They'll be sorry when I'm dead'? But, setting aside strong, finely integrated spirits like our own, let us admit that in nineteenth-century audiences there were people who had a considerable gallonage of self-pity contained within them; for the men it was broached when some splendid fellow laid down his life for a friend or for the woman he loved; for women the floodgates opened when a misunderstood woman who, for all her faults, was a splendid creature, found understanding, pity, forgiveness, and true happiness only at the threshold of the tomb. The theatre is the Mirror of Nature, and self-pity is a rarely acknowledged aspect of nature.

Froufrou came to grief because all her life she was treated as a child, a toy, and understandably she traded on that false character until she was brought face to face with another kind of reality. The date of the play is 1869. It was just ten years later that another child-wife, a little sky-lark, a little squirrel, was betrayed by the false character that had been forced upon her, and came to grief, but gained the strength by her experience to break out of her doll's house and face the world and the very slight chance that a miracle will save her marriage. What a howl there was! Hamburg and Vienna demanded a happy ending; Norah must not slam the door, she must yield to the need of her innocent children. Even the giant Ibsen had to yield to this demand. But in *A Doll's House*, twenty years before the full onset of the Freudian Revolution, we see the explosion of the earlier Romanticism, and the coming of a new kind of psychological truth that was with uttermost difficulty manifesting itself in literature and finding some echoes in life itself. For Ibsen, there is no refuge in Heroine's Disease.

Ibsen is, of course, a genius of the highest order, and through his insight into the truer nature of woman he did much to free women from falsities that had long plagued them. Not that Ibsen ever considered himself a feminist; he detested rancorous female revolutionaries. But he had in the highest degree the ability of a literary genius to see through a brick wall – a wall of popularly accepted psychology and self-interested prejudice.

Norah Helmer is by no means his only portrait of a woman who comes to grips with what popular psychology has done to her. Hedda Gabler has to face the bitterness of being a small-town enchantress who is beaten at her own game by a woman she despises. Ellida Wangel, in *The Lady From the Sea*, has to set aside her cherished romantic dreams of an ideal lover for the reality of her situation. Ibsen holds the mirror up to a new sort of nature, in which is reflected a world where women are freer, and also more responsible than they have been. Dying will not solve their problems, though Hedda kills herself, thinking perhaps that Tesman and Mrs Elvsted and Judge Brack will be sorry for what she has done – as of course they will be, for a while, but not one imagines for very long. Striking one set of shackles from women, Ibsen replaces them with another and perhaps even heavier set – the necessity to accept responsibility for one's own actions.

When that has been said, however, we have to admit that these heroines of Ibsen's do not wholly content us. For good or ill, men will go on idealizing women, and acceptance of total responsibility for their actions and a keen undeluded mind are not the only attractions women may have. Bernard Shaw has given us women who have that sort of attraction, and though we are delighted with them in his comedies they have no life elsewhere. One of the oddities of criticism is that there are still people who think that Shaw was a follower and disciple of Ibsen, when manifestly he was nothing of the sort. Ibsen's women have their roots deep in the new psychology that fired the Freudian Revolution; like icebergs, six-sevenths of them is below the surface. Shaw's women live very much in the sun; like their creator, they are fountains of wit and superficially revolutionary thought, but seem wholly unaware of what was new in the world of the spirit, which Freud demonstrated. Ibsen's women have abundant life: one can imagine them without their clothes, or growing old, or being ill. Shaw's women are all in obstreperous mental and physical health, but like dolls their clothes do not come off, and their speech, though often brilliant, never evokes chivalrous or poetic feeling.

Is it then the task of women to evoke chivalrous and poetic feeling? Well, they have done so for many centuries and some of the finest of them have considered it a splendid privilege to do so. They are not usually the wives and mothers, the skylarks and squirrels, the Froufrous and Lady Isabels. They give the impression of knowing things that lie far beyond the ken of such sillies. They are the love-goddesses, and in the nineteenth-century by far the greatest to tread the stage was a character based on the life of a Norman peasant girl who began life as Alphonsine Plessis, which she later changed to Marie Duplessis; the most gifted of her lovers called her Marguerite Gautier, and in the opera in which she still lives, somewhere in the world, during most of every year, she is called Violetta Valéry. She was *La Dame aux camélias* (1852) and the English version of the play about her, which has been translated many times, is called *Camille*.

Although she owes much to the portrait of her that was presented by Alexandre Dumas the Younger, we have the assurance of many other men who loved her that he did not exaggerate her extraordinary fascination. Countless actresses have sought to recreate that fascination on the stage, with more or less success. The secret of playing the role, some of its finest exponents have assured us, lies not in pumping up feminine fascination with the anxious energy of a sailor pumping bilge, but in repose. This it was, combined with her wistful beauty, which enslaved the young Dumas. She was not a woman of commanding talents in the Shavian sense; she could play the piano and sing, but not uncommonly well; she was an amusing talker, but the examples of her wit that survive do not strike us mute;

absurd though the comparison may seem, she was like Falstaff, in that she was the cause of wit in others, and evoked whatever was best or most characteristic in them. In the terms of Jungian psychology, she constellated the archetype of the Anima in the men who loved her; she was the living embodiment of an ideal, more splendid than they had ever dreamed that ideal might be. In the terms of the world of Courtly Love, she was Lady Soul.

Now, Lady Soul is not a religious concept. She is desirable and she may be attained. Marguerite, or Violetta to use the name Verdi attached to her, was attainable because she was a courtesan, an hetaera, and she was very, very expensive.

When the play was translated into English, and particularly when it was translated for American presentation by the eminently respectable Matilda Heron, Marguerite's station in life gave immense difficulty, because the concept of the courtesan was so foreign to the American mind at that time. A woman who was kept by a man, or by several men at once, was plainly a whore. The concept of the hetaera did not accord readily with nineteenth-century puritanism. So Marguerite's source of livelihood had to be kept as vague as possible, and insofar as it was suggested at all, she was made to be deeply remorseful about it, and to make it clear that her way of life was not of her choosing.

We know better, and the novels of Balzac give us

a detailed account of the sort of life Marguerite lived, and the understandings it involved, and the high finance that was its underpinning. Courtesans allowed men to pay their bills, provide them with luxurious dwellings and carriages, and sustain them in the most extravagant sort of life that cities like Paris afforded. But this did not make the courtesan the financier's property; his share in her favours was carefully delineated, and sometimes part of his expense was a generous allowance for the real lover of the girl, who might be a man of limited fortune. The courtesan was a fashionable accoutrement of a millionaire's manner of life, just as he might own a yacht or a stable of racehorses, without himself expecting either to steer the yacht or ride the horses. The courtesan was a symbol of affluence. But she could be, and Camille was, an extraordinary enlargement of life.

Dumas, who was not affluent, broke off his romance with Marie Duplessis because he could not bear to play the part of a kept man. In the novel this is made plain; in the play it is made even plainer; in the opera we may be said to catch it on the fly, amid a complex of other involvements. But these are the peripheral facts of the story of the Lady of the Camellias; the truth lies in the transporting quality of the romance, and that springs from what Marguerite was, and what she could evoke in a poet who loved her.

This is one of the most difficult emotional complexes to make manifest in art, and when it is achieved it is of never-failing fascination. Young love, lost love, and the spell of the Lost Lady – the desirable woman, a part of whose charm lies in her blemished but poetic nature – are themes that the minor dramatists of the nineteenth century could not evoke with any strength, and which did not lie even in the formidable range of Ibsen or Shaw. The Lost One – the Erring One – La Traviata – the spell of this figure is explicable in Freudian terms, even more sympathetically in Jungian terms – but it is not explanations we ask for: the spell is numinous and stirring, and should not be broken. It is a great theme of art, because it is an inescapable fact of life.

Tomorrow I shall say something about the comedy of the nineteenth-century theatre, and as comedy is under discussion it will involve some consideration of nineteenth-century ideas about sex. But I shall also speak of a figure that, in psychological terms, has a place in our consciousness, and that is the figure of the Doomed or Fated Man, the man subsumed in melancholy and remorse, as he manifests himself in the long, romantic journey toward the Freudian Revolution.

LECTURE THREE

My Cue is Villainous Melancholy

IN THESE LECTURES I do not like to stray far, or for long, from my principal theme, which is the Mirror of Nature. For our purposes I have defined nature as what seems to be nature to the theatre audience – that is to say, whatever is acceptable, credible, not luring the spectators into realms that have no meaning in terms of their own lives. But, as I said at the beginning, during the nineteenth century the concept of what was nature in this sense changed from the psychology current during the eighteenth century to the depth psychology of Sigmund Freud, as these things were understood by the generality of playgoers. There were people going to the theatre in 1825 who were, if such thoughts ever troubled them, still attached to psychological ideas that were current in 1775, and certainly there were people in audiences in 1925 who were still thinking about mankind in terms of 1875. But not everybody needs to subscribe to a new concept to make it part of the perceived wisdom of its time, and though many dallied by the way, the change from 1800 to 1900 may be described as a change from the last of Classicism to the well-established, negative, egotistical but still powerfully Romantic outlook which we have been developing and in some respects refining ever since.

Psychology, in our sense of the term, hardly existed for the Neo-Classicists, for they dealt in general concepts rather than subjective personal responses. But they had their ideas about how the human mind worked, and, however strange these may seem to us, we must accord them the respect owing to ideas which bore meritorious fruit. One of these notions which the psychology of our time has wholly discarded may be called the exclusive power of the passions. That is to say, only one strong emotion might possess the mind at one time; the wars between jealousy and pity, or love and hate, with which we experience no difficulty were not Classical. The whole scheme of this sort of thinking is well summed up in William Collins' 'Ode on the Passions,' written in 1747, which elocutionists loved to impose upon their hearers until about 1850. It is elegant in its simplicity, and simplistic in its elegance. The Passions were Fear, then Anger with his eyes on fire, then Despair which was 'sad by fits, by starts 'twas wild,' and then came Hope; there followed Revenge, who 'threw his blood-stained sword in thunder down,' then Pity, who was characterized as 'dejected,' followed by Jealousy: – 'now it courted love, now raving called on hate'; then came pale Melancholy; Melancholy was succeeded by Cheerfulness, 'A nymph of healthiest hue,' in whose train you will be pleased to know —

Brown Exercise rejoiced to hear,
And sport leapt up and seized his beechen spear.

Understandably this was followed by Joy, then Love, and finally Mirth, who seems to have been a very jolly Passion for we are told that 'Loose were her tresses seen, her zone unbound.' As you see, there were six laudable Passions which might be indulged decorously but gladly, and six evil Passions, which brought unhappy consequences.

It is a system for defining the aspects of the mind and, like so many systems, it flies in the face of common experience. One of the things from which Freud and Jung have delivered us is belief in psychological systems of any mechanical or generally applicable sort. What totally routed the eighteenth-century system of the Passions was Romanticism, which draws so much of its power from its recognition that several passions, including some not named among Collins' twelve, may possess the mind at once.

Romanticism swept through nineteenth-century popular sensibility like a fire, and was — and still is — powerful even when distressingly vulgarized. To say that it came from Germany is too easy a generalization. It is interesting, nevertheless, to read that at midnight, on 31 December 1799, in the Court of Weimar, a group of German writers led by Goethe and Schiller toasted the dawn of a new literature. What followed is well known. In 1800 Schiller's *Maria Stuart* appeared, the theme of which is the romantic one of victory plucked from defeat, and an unhappy destiny as a path to sublimity of feeling and conduct. Goethe's *Faust*, a work of incalculable influence in European thought, appeared in its first part in 1808, and was concluded in the author's advanced age in 1832. There used to be people who said it was unactable, but I have seen both parts splendidly staged in Germany and it is magnificent theatre. In France the revolutionary break with Neo-Classic, pseudo-Aristotelian convention was led by Victor Hugo, with *Ernani* in 1830, *Le Roi S'Amuse* in 1832, and *Ruy Blas* in 1838, all exalting the mighty soul which might not necessarily be associated with noble birth, and exploiting that huge, widespread sense of having been ill-used, that leaning toward self-pity, which is one of the most resonant strings in the Romantic lyre.

Of course this revolution does not fit neatly into a chronological scheme. Nineteen years before *Maria Stuart* Schiller had written his Romantically revolutionary play, *Die Raüber*, and certainly France was not dead to the appeal of romance until Hugo created his theatre explosion. History of art or science does not advance neatly under chronological banners.

There were no works to compare with the European masterpieces in the English-speaking theatre with which we are chiefly concerned. The trouble was partly economic; writing plays in England and in America was sweated labour to which writers of proven worth would not stoop. But there was something else: too many of the great writers in English – Wordsworth, Coleridge, and Shelley, to name but three – were so bamboozled by a German example which they only partly understood, and so dominated by the voice of Shakespeare, which they could not get out of their heads, that they wrote what are simply bad imitative plays in which there are nuggets of good poetry. Byron could rid himself of the Shakespeare bugaboo, but he was incapable of learning anything from anyone, and writing plays is an art that must be practised in collaboration with many other artists,and particularly actors, who are a wilful people. They are so used to assuming the outward aspect of anything that nothing will deter them from assuming the role of author for which they are only rarely psychologically fitted. Nevertheless, they have secrets to impart to an author, of which the most powerful is that there are moments when a silence is worth thirty lines of verse. Our great poets, when they attempted to write for the stage, wrote with a wholly undisciplined profusion.

The English plays of the nineteenth century are extremely numerous, and they are, in the main, undistinguished by literary merit, though many of them are not nearly so bad as people who have not studied them suppose. There is a lesson to be learned from them which is uncomfortable, if you happen to consider drama a branch of literature. It is this: plays of modest literary worth have sometimes been remarkably successful on the stage, pleasing some of the ablest critics of their time over fifty, sixty, seventy, and occasionally a hundred years of presentation. People whose opinion we cannot brush aside have attested to their power. They awoke responses in their audiences which we cannot understand simply by studying the texts. And here we must remember the Mirror of Nature: these plays spoke to nineteenth-century playgoers of things that lay ready to be evoked, of feelings that could be brought to the surface and indulged when the right mood was created. Who created the mood? The actors, far more than the authors, and we cannot think of this theatre without according the actors their proper place.

The nineteenth century was very much the age of the virtuoso. In the arts of music and theatre, audiences loved those performers who were technically astounding and of extraordinary, evocative personal style. Paganini raising the Devil on his violin; Franz Liszt beating the piano as it had never been beaten before; Berlioz conducting like a man possessed; and in the theatre the fiery genius of Edmund Kean, the furies of Macready, and the saint-and-devil alternations of Henry Irving were what, in their own phrase, fetched them. Only when the century was nearing its end was there any strong call for a milder naturalism. For the greater part of the century audiences found nature mirrored in the artistic efforts of extraordinary people. Even when naturalism seemed to have won the fight, the uncommon, the remarkable, the heaven-storming, never lost its power. We have enjoyed in this century about fifty years of acting by some great practitioners of that art, and they have never lacked for enthusiastic audiences, for the greatest drama, like the greatest music, does not yield to the approaches of modest, unilluminated performers. We have found that even Ibsen and Shaw, once hailed as realists, demand a Classical equipment if they are to be played with full effect. It was after all in the nineteenth century that Goethe said that art is art because it is not natural; no, it only seems natural because it speaks to the depths.

Of course it is possible to make a case for a measure of realism in nineteenth-century theatre by discussing the work of T.W. Robertson and many writers of merit who learned from him. But theirs was a realism of surfaces; they reflected the outward aspects of life. The inner life, the life of the spirit, remained with a different sort of play and a wholly different class of player. And what is nature? Is it the surface, or the core? The argument could be a long one, and as I have chosen to speak chiefly of melodrama, I must choose the core. The greatest art brings us near to the archetypal ideas themselves, and not, as Yeats says, toward nature, which is but their looking-glass. Goethe and Yeats, both men of the theatre, understood this profound truth as Wordsworth, Shelley, and Coleridge did not.

In the first of these lectures I spoke of some of the themes of melodrama in the early part of the century. They were the themes which, refined in treatment, held their power until 1900, and long afterward. But beyond that date I must not stray; I will say, however, that in such modern successful plays as *Equus* and *Amadeus* melodrama lives on, for it is not merely a style of writing, it is a mode of living and perceiving life. With its freedom to include both comedy and tragedy, pathos and irony, and to come to conclusions which are not solely comic or tragic, it is a mode of perceiving life that is particularly suited to our post-Freudian world.

What themes did it use most often, in the period under discussion? The theme of the Fated Man, whether it is in the high mode of Byron in *Manfred* or the popular mode of *The Vampyre*. The theme of unrecognized merit showing itself superior to external circumstances, in such plays as *The Lady of Lyons* (1838), *Ruy Blas*, or, in a wholly different milieu, *Uncle Tom's Cabin*. It is the theme of the great value that is to be found in the despised, as in *La*

Dame aux camélias or *The Stranger*. It is the theme of renunciation, as in *The Colleen Bawn* (1860) and *The Corsican Brothers*. It is the theme of remorse, as in *The Iron Chest* (1796) and *The Bells* (1871).

If these seem to be several themes, a little consideration reveals that there is an underlying sympathy among them. What is it?

Of course there is the Romantic theme of the supremacy of the individual. Mankind is inescapably egotistical. How can it be otherwise when every human creature experiences everything that comes his way in terms of his own five senses enclosed in his own body? What possible sympathy or understanding can he have for anyone or anything except as it is based on his own perceptions? Egotism, like self-pity, has a bad name, but it is a fact of our existence. With this egotism may very well go a conviction of inner worth, of a fineness which the world does not recognize. Even the humblest may harbour an inner image of a great conqueror, a world philosopher, a saint, or an enchantress, which lurks, concealed from the vulgar gaze, within what seems to be a wholly unremarkable breast. 'Two such men as I would destroy the entire moral structure of the world,' says Karl Moor, in *Die Räuber*. Most of us, happily, control this voice within us; those who cannot, figure in the daily news as assassins and perpetrators of public outrages. But it is one of the privileges of the theatre to make manifest the inadmissible, and to allow us, for the duration of a play, to feel what might happen if we gave rein to something very deep within us.

In these depths, where the Unacknowledged Great Man lurks, there are other elements, deeply felt, but rarely and furtively examined, and one of the most powerful of these is Guilt.

I am not speaking simply of readily comprehensible guilt for obvious sin, though that is important. I am talking about that Universal Guilt which Freud traced to a sexual cause and to which the name of the Oedipus Complex has not very happily been attached; it is unsuitable, of course, because only by elaborate contortion can the plight of Oedipus be given any significance in the psychological character of women, who are roughly half of all mankind. In this matter I prefer the concept of Guilt put forward by Jung, who places it in a much wider landscape. He says: 'There is absolutely no truth that does not spell salvation to one person and damnation to another. All universalisms get stuck in this terrible dilemma' (*Psychology and Alchemy*, paragraph 36). 'Evil needs to be pondered just as much as good, for good and evil are ultimately nothing but ideal extensions and abstractions of doing, and both belong to the chiaroscuro of life.' The theatre in a very special way presents us with this chiaroscuro of life, this perpetual play of light and shade which is deeply personal, and in the theatre people who are not disposed to psychological introspection may, nevertheless, meet the Universal Sense of Guilt, and be enlarged by the encounter. Enlarged, I say, because a recognition of the guilt in oneself is a necessity to psychological wholeness – not goodness, but wholeness, which is a larger concept. And the ambiguity of guilt – the apparent good deed that brings an evil consequence, and the seeming evil deed that bears good fruit – presents a philosophical problem that few of us are able to meet and vanquish.

As well as the generalized sense of guilt, there is, of course, guilt for particular acts of commission or omission, and these assert themselves in the theatre in extremely interesting forms. I said earlier that in the theatre tragedy or drama tends to deal with what is most profoundly felt, and that comedy often plays dangerously with matters that are greatly feared. The way in which the nineteenth-century theatre deals with matters of sex offers a most interesting study.

The strict policing of sexual references and involvements which is sometimes spoken of as Victorianism had its beginning long before Queen Victoria's birth. It is an aspect of Romanticism. Women, in eighteenth-century drama, are pretty well divided into the women of comedy, who are somewhat superficially observed but who are endowed with common sense and frequently with wit, and the women of tragedy, who have as profound a sensibility as the dramatist is able to provide. They are moved by sex in terms of the manners and ideas of their time, but they are not prurient. With the coming of Romanticism a prurience makes its appearance which only a gifted writer can conceal for what it is. The comedy heroines of nineteenth-century plays greatly enjoy being in love, their principal aim in life is to get married, and if they achieve that within the confines of the play, they sometimes appear with a baby. But of sexual feeling, or the complexity of sexual involvement which is the stuff of so much of the world's great comedy, there is nothing at all. Novelists contrived to get around this prohibition, and a heedful reading of Dickens or Thackeray, or of Anthony Trollope, can be an eye-opener to the reader who finds none of the explicit descriptions of sexual experience that are common in our day. Dickens seems to have taken the line that if you cannot guess what fate awaits Florence Dombey when, as a little girl, she falls into the clutches of Good Mother Brown, it is probably better that you should not know and it is not his intention to risk his livelihood by telling you. But on the stage such broad hints have to be reduced to sly winks. And so the girls of comedy become either simpletons and gigglers, or else little toughs whose chief interest in life is money. And their mothers and their unmarried aunts become caricatures and Gorgons.

In melodrama, as I have already said, women are either Vessels of the Honour of the hero, without any discernible character of their own, or they are villainesses, whose wickedness is obviously compounded by sexual experience, or soiled doves, who may be redeemed by a good man's love, rather as in our time a member of the Humane Society scrapes the heavy oil from the plumage of a seagull; of course, it remains a dirty bird, unless it has the good grace to die, and thereby clean itself up for good.

In what I am now about to say I wish to be as moderate as is proper in uttering generalities that are by their nature incapable of complete proof. I suggest that a substantial amount of the underlying guilt among playgoers, male and female, in the nineteenth century, had its origin in the thoroughly unrealistic attitude toward sex to which I have made reference. Officially, it was asserted that the uttermost propriety was the norm of society. The medical science of the day, not only in England but in America and on the Continent, asserted that a woman of good character had little if any sexual physical sensation or desire, and that such feeling in a woman was morbid in the medical sense of the word. Young women were presumed to be largely ignorant of their own physiology until they married. This was the attitude which dictated the tone and subject-matter of the drama, and especially of comedy.

Such an attitude existed side by side with the fact that prostitutes regularly haunted theatres in search of clients, and rubbed shoulders with the virtuous in the lobbies, where they must have been recognizable. London during that century is reckoned to have housed between fifty and eighty thousand prostitutes – higher than the modern figure. Houses of prostitution were numerous, and there were houses of homosexual prostitution and houses for sadists and masochists as well. Child prostitution was common. The domestic atmosphere of – I will not say purity, because purity and ignorance are not the same thing – seems to have created a dullness that drove men to find livelier women. Popular song of the era gets as near to the truth as the age dared to go. Listen to this, from mid-century:

> Oh, I met her on a steamer
>   As I journeyed to Cremorne,
> A crinoline and a pork-pie hat
>   Her figure did adorn;
> Our glances met, she smiled at me,
>   Then, as if unawares,
> My arm it slipped around her waist,
>   While on the cabin stairs,
> I asked her if she'd go with me,
>   Said she, 'Yes, if I'd let her,'

'Twas just as good as going home,
      Yes, as Good, and a Good Deal Better.

Women, you see, were supposed not to know a great many things men knew, which is always a trouble-making state of affairs. Men, if they were gentlemen, learned about sex at school, and they learned from the most respected instructors – the Greek and Latin classics. In *Don Juan* Byron tells us that

> *Ovid's a rake, as half his verses show him,*
>   *Anacreon's morals are a still worse sample,*
> *Catullus scarcely has a decent poem,*
>   *I don't think Sappho's Ode a good example.*

We now know a good deal about the pornographic literature of the period, and we have autobiographies such as *My Life* that throw light on the unacknowledged sexual life of, it appears, great numbers of people in all ranks of society. Hypocrisy was an inevitable consequence of the social code, and hypocrisy is fertile soil for guilt. Not necessarily guilt for specific sexual misdemeanour, though we cannot suppose that the condition of affairs in a great many boarding-schools left every man untouched, but a broader guilt about the facts of contemporary life, and the idealized world presented on the stage. The silly girls and women of nineteenth-century comedy and farce represent an ideal which could not be squared with fact, and art was made the pander to a special degree of prurience.

Part of the disillusion expresses itself in the disagreeable portraits of middle-aged women and especially unmarried women that are a part of these plays. The sexual desire that is denied to the pure young girl is often exhibited in a gross form in the characters of old maids, who may be monsters of contorted virtue, or even – and W.S. Gilbert is a notable offender in this respect – man-hungry harpies, ravening for husbands. There is an ugly juvenility about this sort of comedy. But what do you expect from a society that equates ignorance with virtue and conspires to treat half the human race as untrustworthy cretins?

Of course there were writers of comedy who did better than this. In the early part of our period there were some who retained the charm and sparkle of the eighteenth century. Toward the end of the century Pinero produced many excellent farces in which sexual matters are lightly and delicately shadowed. But such writers were writing comedy in which one of the most comic elements in nature is taboo. They were brilliantly making bricks without straw. They were holding the mirror up, not to nature in the larger sense, but to the perverted nature of a special age.

The revulsion with which the nineteenth century met anything which, however true or deeply felt, was considered 'unwholesome' in the sexual realm was strikingly exemplified in the horror with which it greeted William Hazlitt's *Liber Amoris* in 1823. In it Hazlitt – no pornographer, you will admit – writes of his pitiful infatuation with Sarah Walker, his landlady's daughter. He is explicit, but not prurient. Psychologically, though not physically, he strips himself naked, as the fool of one aspect of love. It is pitiable and profound in its psychological exploration. And oh! how his contemporaries loathed it – in some cases, surely, because they felt its terrible, unfashionable truth.

What about the serious drama? It is here that the shadow of Guilt is darkest. I do not want to get into trouble with the theologians when I talk of Guilt, but I must repeat that I mean that profound sense of unworthiness, of not having behaved well in all circumstances, of guilt shared with mankind, or a nation, or a group because certain manifest injustices and inadequacies are part of life. There lies deep in the human spirit a well of melancholy with which virtually everyone who has any inner life at all is acquainted. When a character on the stage says or hints 'My cue is villainous melancholy' he touches a deep note, a pedal point, in the harmony of life and extraordinary developments may emerge in that harmony.

'Gorgons and Hydras, and Chimaeras – dire stories of Celaeno and the Harpies – may reproduce themselves in the brain of superstition – but they are there before. They are transcripts, types – the archetypes are in us, and eternal.' Who said that? Was it Jung? No, it was Charles Lamb, who knew as much about melancholy and all that is involved in it as any man of the nineteenth century. Men and women who may be contemptuous of introspection as an unwholesome indulgence, who never read poetry or novels or history that might arouse more than superficial images of life, may very well be theatregoers. Seated comfortably in box, pit, or gallery they feel positive pleasure when they are brought face to face with the Gorgon whose hideous countenance petrifies those who assail her, but which achieves a wondrous beauty in death: such playgoers well know the struggle with the Hydra, which, like the inadmissible temptings of sex, is no sooner robbed of one head than another appears in its place: both men and women know the Harpy Celaeno, who fouls the very food on the domestic hearth and makes life a burden: they have been forced to encounter the Chimaera, and, if they are lucky, they have a Pegasus to ride in the fight with the fiery monster. These mythological creatures are not simply the artistic creations of our fanciful ancestors; they are attempts, and very successful attempts, to give concrete form to a positive life-problem; they represent the psychological insight of a remote but by no means naive society. They are not the preserve of the educated class, for they represent universal problems, knowing no bounds of literacy or refinement. They are the matrices in which human experience is formed; they are the Mothers, shown to Faust in a moment of extraordinary revelation.

And they are, of course, the stuff of powerful theatrical experience.

We have already spoken of some of these archetypal figures – of Frankenstein's Monster, for instance, whose instincts are good and even noble, but whose hideous form turns mankind against him. And Manfred, the best example of so many Fated Men, whose love brings destruction in its train; Ruthven, in *The Vampyre* is a cruder manifestation of the same type. In *The Lady of Lyons* (1838) the gardener's gifted son proves, in the new world brought forth by Napoleon, to be the superior of those who sought to use him basely, and in particular the girl who thought he was not good enough for her. Any echoes there? Any gentleman present who has not, at some time, met a girl who thought he was not good enough for her, and preferred a manifest idiot? The same feeling of high romance pervades *Ruy Blas*, where the valet loves a Queen and shows that, in a judgement better than that of this world, he is indeed a worthy knight. In *Uncle*

Tom's Cabin we meet the Suffering Servant, the great soul undervalued, a type familiar in literature from the Old Testament to Eeyore the Donkey; and in this same play, in Little Eva St Clair, we meet the very powerful archetypal figure of the Miraculous Child, who brings blessing to all who come into its orbit. In *The Stranger* and *La Dame aux camélias* we meet the Lost Lady, a sinner transfigured by suffering, so powerful that, when Sarah Bernhardt played Camille before Queen Victoria, that stern judge of morals said. 'You play the part with modesty, and no one can complain.' In *The Colleen Bawn*, and *The Corsican Brothers*, and of course in that famous melodrama based on *The Tale of Two Cities* – *The Only way* (1899) – we have the theme of Renunciation, of the man whose love for the darling of his heart is so great that he resigns her to a man she loves better than he, thereby showing himself a nobler creature than either of the pair he has made happy.

There are female counterparts for all of these themes, though I have spoken only of *Camille*, and *Froufrou*, a tale of self-sacrifice. All the successful examples of such plays are fountains of that melancholy which, though painful, may also be healing to the spirit.

Melancholy in itself is a passive indulgence. Unless it is united with a secret cause it is not the stuff of drama. Nineteenth-century drama abounds in men with guilty secrets, and the fact that it found such enthusiastic response in its audiences makes us wonder if there were not a great many men with guilty secrets in private life. It is a curious circumstance about the possession of a guilty secret that the possessor so often feels impelled to hint at it – to trail his cloak, as it were. Is there any more extraordinary instance of this in the world of theatre than that we find in the case of Oscar Wilde who, at the height of his fame, wrote *Lady Windermere's Fan. A Woman of No Importance, An Ideal Husband,* and *The Importance of Being Earnest,* all of which are about men with secrets, sometimes serious and sometimes not; it is as though he could not refrain from hinting that he too possessed a secret, the secret which brought about his ruin.

The melancholy hero and his discreditable secret run right through the nineteenth-century theatre. Colman's curious drama *The Iron Chest* was first seen on the stage in 1796 and it continued to be a favourite with strongly dramatic actors at least until 1879, when Henry Irving gave it a notable production. As a play it is a dreadful muddle, for it combines comedy, tragedy, and something like opera in an uneasy union. The comedy is not incidental relief to the tragic action, but a substantial factor in the play itself. The music, by Storace, is sufficiently prominent and quite good enough to demand attention for its own sake. But the tragic action is so intense that it overbears the other two elements, however, uneasily it seems to be integrated with them.

The story is of a man, Sir Edmund Mortimer, virtuous and admired as a just and merciful ruler of the New Forest. 'He is one of those judges who, in their office, will never warp the law to save offenders; but his private charity bids him assist the needy, before their necessity drives them to crimes, which his public duty must punish,' says one of the characters. Obviously, then, a good and upright man, but he suffers fits of remorse which are linked with evidence contained in an iron chest in his library. In time we discover that he had, in the past, inadvertently killed an enemy – a despicable tyrant, but the uncle of the woman he loves – and this drives him to further shameful deeds until at last, in a dreadful scene of guilt disclosed, he dies, presumably of remorse.

Incredible? Apparently not when, for instance, the great Edmund Kean played it. There is a story that on one occasion, when he was playing Mortimer in the provinces, one of the supporting actors asked him if, as the actor was familiar with his role, it was necessary for him to rehearse with Kean. It should be explained that in those days (it was about 1820) leading actors went on tour in the provinces, playing their most famous roles with the local companies, who were already acquainted with the play to be performed; it is a system that still persists in the world of opera, where a visiting star may rehearse only once or twice with the local company. To the actor who asked if there were any need for him to rehearse something he already knew, Kean said, 'Have you ever seen me in this drama, Sir?' and the daring actor said he had not. 'Then you had better rehearse,' said Kean, 'for by God, sir, I will *terrify* you!'

How did he terrify his fellow actors and the audiences? His first biographer says, 'He did not exhibit much spasm; nor did he roar out the confession of his murder, like the bull of Bāshan; but he *looked*! – as no one ever looked, before or since. The tones of his voice, trembling with remorse, penetrated your heart; and in the trial scene, where he sat silent, and death-pale, his fingers grasping the arm-chair in which he sat, till you thought that the strong oak must crumble into powder – who has ever done the like?' (Barry Cornwall [Procter] *The Life of Edmund Kean*, 2 volumes, London 1835.)

It was the power of acting, with players of the stamp of Kean and Irving, that made this jumble of comedy and music and drama memorable as the tragedy of a stricken soul; it is significant that it was his terrible quietness, rather than any inexplicable dumb-shows and noise, that made the fall of Mortimer dreadful to see. This was the power of the virtuoso performer.

When we think of a nineteenth-century tragedian we may recall Bernard Shaw's admiring descriptions of Barry Sullivan, who could roar astonishingly, and strike awe into his listeners by the sheer power of elocution. But it was not noise that marked the greatest actors of the age, but their silences and their evocation of a terror that might well be fatal.

The seeming poor quality of the plays in which these effects were produced has disgusted scholars who forget, or cannot conceive of, the great acting, and has led them to suppose that our nineteenth-century ancestors were naive in the theatre to a degree that certainly does not show itself in their responses to poetry or the novel. But are these plays so poor? They do not stand up to Aristotelian analysis, certainly, but they have a quality which we can still discover, and be thrilled by, in opera.

Consider Verdi's *Il Trovatore*. There are musical scholars who would like to forget it, as unworthy of Verdi, not because the music is ineffective, but because the libretto is a jumble of recollected crime, vengeance, thwarted love, and extreme heroics in which there is no development of character, and in which the plot defies logical analysis. *But the thing works*; when it is finely and sincerely performed it thrills its audiences and they are, for the time, unheeding of its failures to meet standards which were never meant to be applied to it. Bernard Shaw, a stringent critic of opera and a valiant fighter for the psychologically superior Wagner, declares that *Il Trovatore* is 'a perfect work of instinct.' That is to say, it triumphs over critical objections by sheer force of emotional vigour and power of execution. To put that in another way, it appeals to that unconscious realm in the audience where critical concepts of credibility and artistic chastity have no authority, and so to speak, goes right to the solar plexus. When criticism ceases to take heed of the immediate emotional appeal of a work of art, and calls upon every work to meet certain abstract conditions or be condemned, it may be that criticism presumes beyond its place in the artistic world. It is the first aim of the virtuoso not to please critics, but to awe them into silence and acceptance. This is another way of meeting the requirements of art. Critics define but do not advance the boundaries of art, which is what the virtuoso seeks to do.

There were many plays that allowed actors of extraordinary abilities to create something that does not seem to be communicated very strongly in the text. One such was Casimir Delavigne's *Louis XI*, (1855), which is as inexplicable in its plot as *Il Trovatore* but which, in the character of the cruel, treacherous old king, terrorized by his hourly expectation of death, gave actors a chance to make the blood freeze, and also to glory in that seemingly inexhaustible variety of human character, the revelation of which is one of the tasks, and glories, of dramatic art.

A play of this kind – that is to say, a scaffold on which a great actor erected an edifice of virtuosity and terrifying emotion, was *The Bells*, which made Henry Irving's name in 1871, and kept him at the top of the theatrical profession until his death in 1905. He played the role of the remorseful innkeeper Mathias more than eight hundred times. I have met many people who saw it, some of them excellent judges of theatrical art, and I have never met anyone who hesitated to describe it in superlative terms, as very great acting.

The play is not bad, but it is unremarkable, and there is not a single line that is memorable on its own account in the translation Leopold Lewis made from the French original by Erckmann and Chatrian. Fifteen years before the action begins an Alsatian innkeeper, Mathias, who stood on the brink of ruin, murdered a Polish Jew who passed through his village, and seized a quantity of gold, upon which he founded his subsequent fortune. When the play begins in the inn parlour, a storm is raging outside, and the villagers remark that it is the worst since what has come to be called the Polish Jew's winter. The innkeeper, Mathias, returns from a neighbouring village where he has been to buy a wedding-gift for his daughter, and when he hears the talk of the evil winter of fifteen years before, he is inexplicably agitated. We know, though his companions do not, that he hears far off the Polish Jew's sleighbells which from time to time ring in his ears and remind him of his crime. He goes to bed, and in a dream he finds himself in a mysterious court, rather like a court in Kafka, where he is on trial for the murder of the Polish Jew; under the influence of a Mesmerist he is made to act out the murder as he committed it, and he is found guilty as the dream closes. When his wife and friends come in the morning to rouse him, wondering why he has slept so late on his daughter's wedding-day, they find him dying of terror as, in his imagination, he is hanged for his crime.

In the telling this seems to be what Gilbert might call a bald and unconvincing narrative. We have plenty of evidence, and especially Gordon Craig's magnificent evocation in prose, of exactly what Irving did and how he did it, which gives us some shadow of an idea of what the audiences who saw Irving underwent, when his spell was upon them. We have also, now, a reprint of Irving's version of the text, with details of the stage management of the production, which helps people who have had stage experience to create something of the original in the theatre of the mind. What Irving evoked was sheer terror, and a sense of guilt that brought a true dramatic catharsis, in his richly detailed, splendidly imaginative, and inventive, portrait of the man whose nemesis grew from the recollected sound of sleighbells to a conviction of guilt too vivid to be borne.

The Bells is sophisticated drama compared with *The Iron Chest* or *Louis XI*. It strikes into those depths of the human mind where incoherent terror lies, and gives that terror voice. But it is still so much in the grip of the Romantic mode that lived throughout the nineteenth century that it deals with only one character in any detail; the others are shadows compared to Mathias. But as the century grew older psychological insight, slow though it was and impeded by the dead weight of intellectual inertia, reached the point where it became clear that nobody is guilty alone, that human tragedy does not concern one extraordinary character and a collection of puppets, and that the complexity of human affairs could not be contained in such dramas, even when virtuoso actors performed them. The dramatist who dared to show us on the stage that when affairs go wrong all are in some degree guilty and that, in Jung's words, 'There is absolutely no truth that does not spell salvation to one person and damnation to another' (*Psychology and Alchemy*, paragraph 36) was Henrik Ibsen, and he had completed his work before Freud and Jung had described, in psychological terms, so much that lies at the root of it.

I have come to disturb the sleep of the world, said Sigmund Freud. Ibsen was a quarter of a century before him in sounding that alarm. The guilt Ibsen shows us is not that of secrets kept in iron chests, or murders upon which future fortune is built, but the guilt of lies in which everybody agrees to conspire, and murders which are not of the body but of the spirit. Not the worst revelation, but the one which caused the greatest outcry among conventional people, was Ibsen's remorseless exposure of the innumerable lies about sex, which slowly and painfully demolished the pretty castles of irrationality that the nineteenth century had agreed to call comedy.

It would be chronologically tidy to speak of Ibsen in terms of his last play, *When We Dead Awaken*, which appeared in 1899, at the close of our century. But we have been talking about plays which deal with the fate of extraordinary men, and the change in emphasis Ibsen gave them, in comparison with such a drama as *The Bells*. Consider *The Master Builder*, of 1892; its hero, Solness, is a man of extraordinary powers which have lifted him to eminence in his profession as a great builder, even though he has had no conventional training. He has no secret, no oppressive sense of guilt, but we see his guilt. His ambition has reduced his wife to a shadow because she and all she has have been absorbed in his career. He has superseded the man who, in his ambitious youth, gave him his start, and he is not kind to this man nor is he ready to give this man's son the chance

that was once given to him. Oh yes, Bygmester Solness is guilty of a very common sin, the sin of belief
in himself carried to the point of unfeeling egotism.
But it is a secret only from himself.

His own downfall appears in the form of a young
woman of charm and great spirit, Hilda Wangel.
The Master Builder is enchanted by her, and in
ways that are painful to watch he attempts to forget
the gulf of years that lies between them. Hilda Wangel is no delightful girl from nineteenth-century
comedy; she has a troll-like spirit of mischief and
destruction, and she tempts the Master Builder to
a folly, because she tests him beyond his powers.
Though a great builder, he is a nervous climber
and, when she urges him to climb a tower and put
the wreath on its pinnacle that marks the conclusion
of the building, he falls and is killed.

Nothing about this play is simple. Why is Solness
so deluded? Is Hilda a girl with no sense of reality,
or is she a devil? And beyond these leading characters we see the misery of the wife, which is not
of tragic dimension because so much of what ails
her is because of an innate inferiority of soul; we
see the sad loss of consequence of the Brovik family,
father and son, upon whose declining fortunes the
career of the Master Builder is raised. We see a
complex human situation, rather than a simple theatrical plot and we see how blameworthy, in certain
respects, and yet how trapped in the destiny of in-

nate character, all these people are. There is not much of comfort, but there is much of illumination, in this play.

Another of Ibsen's dramas, one of the greatest and the second to the last in his completed work, which is also a tale of the unusual man who has come to grief because of his exceptional quality, is *John Gabriel Borkman*, the date of which is 1896. Borkman is a financier who has dared greatly, which means, as it so often does with financiers, that he has used money which was not his own and lost it. But Borkman has a dark splendour; he is a crook, but a crook on a big scale, and nothing will ever convince him that he is a crook. He has undergone three years of investigation, followed by five years of jail, and he has spent a further eight years pacing up and down in the great chamber of his mansion, estranged from his wife, who lives downstairs. At last, at the bidding of the woman who has loved him greatly – and who is his wife's twin sister – he leaves his self-imposed imprisonment, and attempts to go once again into the world and re-establish his reputation. But he dies in the snow, and the two women who have loved him and quarrelled over him are reunited over his dead body. Reunited? Never. It is a truce of tigers and we cannot imagine it will last long.

What elements are combined in this extraordinary, wonderful drama! Ibsen, the great precursor of the depth psychologists, displays the richness of his insight in every line of this play. The sister who loved him but did not win him, Ella Rentheim, is dying of a disease which is not named, but which suggests cancer. It had its beginnings, her physician suggests, in a psychological blow of great significance, and we know that it was Borkman who dealt that blow when he refused her love because it would not serve his career. One of Borkman's reproaches to himself is that he did not, when a young man, dare more boldly in love, and risk all by uniting with Ella Rentheim. But in the play we meet his son, Erhart, who is determined to do precisely that; he leaves the responsibilities his father and mother seek to heap upon him to run off with Mrs Wilton, a woman seven years his senior, whom he loves with the desperate devotion of a man of twenty. He is determined, in fact, to live out the unlived portion of his father's life, which sounds hopeful, but which, because of his character and the character of the woman he has idealized, we can see is doomed to end in wretchedness. A character of painful pathos is Borkman's one faithful friend, his old clerk Foldal, whose life is endurable only because he thinks he is a poet, and that his tragedy, over which he has muddled all his life, has merit. It is Borkman, of course, the great egotist who loves truth when it does not concern himself, who tells poor Foldal that the tragedy is worthless. But Foldal has hope, to the last; his darling daughter is going off with Erhart and his beloved, to study music in Italy. Here again we have the pathos of a parent's belief that a child will redress his failure. Foldal never knows that Mrs Wilton is taking Fanny simply as a bone to throw to Erhart if her own romance with him should not work well.

Not, as you see, a cheerful play. Not a jolly evening out for the tired business man. But how envigorating it is! There is something bracing, rather like a sauna, about these plays by Ibsen. As in a sauna, the surroundings are not cheerful; the nakedness is un-Greek and unflattering, and undeniably you roast; the dashes of icy water and the flailings with birch twigs are severe; but when it is all over how clean you feel! In the nineteenth century, however, people did not seek this sauna effect in the theatre, and there was a terrible outcry against Ibsen, just as later there was an outcry against Freud. Both men disturbed the sleep of the world, and that is a dangerous thing to do.

Yet how much we have gained from them. We look at mankind now in quite a different way, and our ideas about the conditional nature of truth and the psychological complexity of human action have been immeasurably extended. We might say, if we were not accustomed to guard our tongues, that Romanticism had at last run its course, and that the cult of the individual which came with the dawn of the nineteenth century had been given a mortal blow when we emerged into the twentieth.

Such easy philosophizing and such belief in the perfectability of mankind and of his theatre will not stand examination. Every age seems to have its presiding genius, its tutelary spirit, and that spirit is something more than the detestation mankind shows for changing its mind. We know that Ellen Terry once tried to interest Henry Irving in producing *John Gabriel Borkman* and playing the lead himself, and we are not surprised that she did not succeed. Ibsen is Romantic – Romantic in the sense that he sees man's fate as a product of personal character. But his is not the flourishing, grotesque Romanticism that Irving understood and of which he was a great virtuoso. It is fruitless to say that if Irving had examined the character of Borkman he would have found much in it to engage his extraordinary understanding of tragedy and the involvements of guilt and ambition, and that his immense abilities would have illuminated the character and the play. To use a colloquial, but apposite, expression, it was simply not in the cards – not merely because it was new but because it did not mirror the sort of nature that had made Irving the greatest actor of his age. 'Teach me to do more than I can,' is Ibsen's cry, not Irving's. The struggle lay in younger hands, which would turn the mirror slightly to reflect a new concept of nature.

One such pair of hands belonged to Bernard Shaw, who was well on his way to fame as our century closes. Shaw was a strong fighter in Ibsen's cause, but can we persuade ourselves that he ever looked for long into the Mirror of Nature that showed Ibsen such a minatory picture of society? Teach me to do more than I can was no more Shaw's cry than it was Irving's. The Freudian Revolution, which Ibsen heralded, seems to have meant little to Shaw, whose outlook on the world, though acerbic, was always that of a writer of comedy, who seemed truly to believe that changed social conditions would alter the nature of humanity. Shaw's temperament is Classic, rather than Romantic, and the Classic temperament is favourable to comedy of ideas and argument, a realm in which Shaw has no rival. But Ibsen's sense of comedy was very different.

The sense of comedy of a great writer is as important in understanding him as his sense of tragedy or pathos. Ibsen's comedy, whatever mitigations we may offer for it, seems harsh and pitiless. But it is not for that reason to be dismissed as not true comedy. In the comedy of the Greeks the same derisive attitude toward fools is apparent, though we may say that Ibsen understands fools more intricately. Ibsen's fools are often the incompetent, the hapless, the ill-equipped for the struggle of life, who nevertheless assert their right, as human beings, to make a mess of their lives and often of other people's lives; Ibsen has little compassion for them, because he sees them as dangerous and their folly as infectious – another aspect of his Freudian insight. People who cannot paddle their own canoe, he seems to say, will certainly sink, and what is pitiable in this demonstration of cause and effect is that they drag down weaker people and children with them. But, as they sink, Ibsen stands on the shore and laughs. It is not an engaging aspect of his genius, but once again it is bracing, especially in a world like our own where incompetence is sometimes accorded a special degree of license, under the general heading of compassion. It is in that painful but hilarious comedy *The Wild Duck* (1884) that we see this terrible castigation of folly by fate in the character of Hjalmar Ekdal, and that prince of fumbling meddlers, Gregers Werle.

Shaw did not share this new perception of the nature of comedy just as he did not share the truly compassionate but piercing comedy of Anton Chekov, whose work also bridges the change from the nineteenth century to the twentieth. Funnier figures than Professor Serebryakov in *Uncle Vanya* (1899), or Gaiev in *The Cherry Orchard* (1904) (who has an hilarious but pitiably ill-founded belief in his capacity to serve the world as a banker) are not to be found in Shaw. Shaw is more genial toward his fools than Ibsen or Chekov; he does not show them remorselessly as mischief-makers and poisoners of the lives of others. Shaw's achievement was, in part, to assist in the revolution which took the theatre away from the great majority of mankind, the revolution brought about by film and now by television, which brings their patrons, so often, much the same sort of romantic world-view that sustained the melodrama of the nineteenth century. Not all the fine talk about film as an art, and the great possibilities of television, can blind us to the procession of cheap romance, of effects that have no persuasive causes, of Poetic Justice, that parades every day across the great screen and the small one. A smear of Freudian and even Jungian insight, degraded to a kind of smart-alec know-it-allism is spread over the great screen and the small one, but the nature they mirror looks like the nature of the past, and the theatre proper has become almost a coterie entertainment, divided unequally between the classics, which the great and the small screen cannot seriously contain, and new plays, which attempt to cultivate Ibsen's rocky field with ploughs that seem sometimes to be no bigger than toothpicks.

Are we to conclude, then, that the nature mirrored in the nineteenth century was the true nature, the inescapable nature? No, we are not required to think anything of the kind. All we are required to do is to recognize that the theatre of the nineteenth century reflected the immensity of nature as well as it could in terms of its time, and that if we condemn what it shows us as unworthy it is because we have failed in imaginative sympathy, a quality without which any understanding either of the theatre as the Mirror of Nature, or of nature herself in all her bewildering and changing variety, is wholly impossible.

As you are by now well aware, my discussion, necessarily selective and imperfect, in these lectures, is an extended plea for imaginative sympathy toward the theatre of the nineteenth century, which was truly, for its time, and in the Shakespearean sense, a Mirror of Nature. But a mirror can only reflect what stands before it, and the person who looks into the mirror can only see what he already knows, or perhaps what he dimly and uneasily suspects. The mirror that was nineteenth-century theatre reflected a change from Neo-Classicism to Romanticism, and from a Romanticism of single heroes and heroines to a Romanticism of families, groups, and societies so harsh and accusatory that it is only by an effort that we recognize it as Romanticism still. But, in the Mirror of Nature that is the theatre, we may be assured that we see – not quite ourselves, but rather what we think of ourselves, which is surely the very age and body of our time, its form and pressure. And as we in our time shall be judged, let us be as understanding as we know how in our judgement of the century gone.

Bibliographical Note

READERS WISHING TO explore the nineteenth-century theatre
will find Volumes IV and V of Allardyce Nicoll's *History of
English Drama* invaluable and Volume VI is the best detailed
list of plays and authors available. Further discussion and
criticism will be found in *The Revels History of Drama in English*,
Volume VI, London 1975, authors Michael R. Booth, Richard
Southern, Frederick and Lise-Lone Marker, and Robertson
Davies. *English Melodrama* by Michael Booth, London 1965,
and *Melodrama* by Willson Disher, London 1954, and *Blood
and Thunder*, London 1949, also by Disher, provide additional
information and opinion.

Texts are more readily available than they were a few years
ago, and Michael Booth's five-volume compilation, *English Plays
of the Nineteenth Century*, Oxford 1969-76, is invaluable. There
are a few anthologies of plays of the period, and for American
examples the reader is referred to *Representative American Plays*,
edited by Arthur Hobson Quinn, New York 1930. Critical
editions of important plays are beginning to make an appearance, and *Henry Irving and the Bells*, Manchester 1980, by
Myer, Jones-Evans and Gardner, gives an excellent essay on
the play, the text of Irving's prompt-book, and the music by
Étienne Singla. The reader who wishes to familiarize himself
with the period, however, should be prepared to read scores
and perhaps hundreds of plays in the original form published
by Lacy, Samuel French, and others who catered to the theatrical
profession and amateurs; these plays are designed for convenience at rehearsal rather than for the library, and the
reader must accustom himself to broken type, usually small
in size, and a maze of stage directions to understand which

he will have to master the theatrical jargon of the time. The reward, however, is great. Collections of plays in this form are to be found in most large libraries.

Books that provide background for the theatrical life of the period are many and of varying dependability. Many actors and managers wrote memoirs, but these are more often endearing works of self-congratulation than documents to be trusted. By reading a great number of them, however, a sense of the period may be attained.

Bearing in mind this caution, the reader will find racy anecdote and lively narrative in *Random Records* by George Colman the Younger, 1830, 2 volumes, and in *The Stage Both Before and Behind the Curtain*, 1840, by the disingenuous Alfred Bunn, playwright, librettist, and manager. *Players and Playwrights I Have Known* by John Coleman, 1888, is full of anecdote of a period long before the date of publication. Insight into the life of one of the most famous players of the century, and an irascible, self-torturing man, will be found in *Diaries of William Charles Macready*, edited in two large volumes by William Toynbee, 1912. Perhaps the best biography of an actor in English, and a fountain of information about the theatre of the nineteenth-century, is *Henry Irving*, written by his grandson Laurence Irving, 1951. Readers curious about the pantomime world will find a delightful introduction to it in *Memoirs of Grimaldi*, edited by Charles Dickens, 1838.

Splendid illumination of the provincial theatre of the early part of the century is to be found in Chapters 22-25, and 29-30, of Dickens' *Nicholas Nickleby*. Vivid detail makes pleasant a reading of *The Life of an Actor* by Pierce Egan, 1825, which is a fictionalized account of the rise to fame of Edmund Kean; the illustrations are invaluable as revelation of the theatrical life of the period.

Nor should the reader neglect *London Labour and the London Poor*, by Henry Mayhew, originally published in 1851, republished in four volumes in 1967: three volumes of excerpts have been edited by Peter Quennel, 1950 and 1951. This is a lively and detailed description of the labouring class for whom so much melodrama was created.

Readers wishing to pursue the psychological path which sometimes appears in the preceding lectures will find in *One Half of Robertson Davies*, Toronto, 1976, in the essay *Jung and the Theatre*, pages 143-160, some discussion of archetypal and dream material that emerges in nineteenth-century popular drama.

THE ALEXANDER LECTURES

The Alexander Lectureship was founded in honour of Professor W.J. Alexander, who held the Chair of English at University College, University of Toronto, from 1889 to 1926. The Lectureship brings to the university a distinguished scholar or critic to give a course of lectures on a subject related to English literature.

1928-9   L.F. Cazamian (Sorbonne): 'Parallelism in the Recent Development of English and French Literature.' Included in *Criticism in the Making* (Macmillan 1929).

1929-30   H.W. Garrod (Oxford): 'The Study of Poetry.' Published as *The Study of Poetry* (Clarendon 1936).

1930-1   Irving Babbitt (Harvard): 'Wordsworth and Modern Poetry.' Included in 'The Primitivism of Wordsworth' in *On Being Creative* (Houghton 1932).

1931-2   W.A. Craigie (Chicago): 'The Northern Element in English Literature.' Published as *The Northern Element in English Literature* (University of Toronto Press 1933).

1932-3   H.J.C. Grierson (Edinburgh): 'Sir Walter Scott.' Included in *Sir Walter Scott, Bart* (Constable, 1938).

1933-4   G.G. Sedgewick (British Columbia): 'Of Irony, Especially in Drama.' Published as *Of Irony, Especially in Drama* (University of Toronto Press 1934).

1934-5   E.F. Stoll (Minnesota): 'Shakespeare's Young Lovers.' Published as *Shakespeare's Young Lovers* (Oxford 1937).

1935-6   Franklin B. Synder (Northwestern), Robert Burns, included in *Robert Burns, His Personality, His Reputation, and His Art* (University of Toronto Press 1936).

1936-7   D. Nichol Smith (Oxford): 'Some Observations on Eighteenth-Century Poetry.' Published as *Some Observations on Eighteenth Century Poetry* (University of Toronto Press 1937).

1937-8   Carleton W. Stanley (Dalhousie): 'Matthew Arnold.' Published as *Matthew Arnold* (University of Toronto Press 1938).

1938-9   Douglas Bush (Harvard): 'The Renaissance and English Humanism.' Published as *The Renaissance and English Humanism* (University of Toronto Press 1939).

1939-41   C. Cestre (Paris): 'The Visage of France.' Lectures postponed because of the war and then cancelled.

1941-2   H.J. Davis (Smith): 'Swift and Stella.' Published as *Stella, A Gentlewoman of the Eighteenth Century* (Macmillan 1942).

1942-3   H. Granville-Barker (New York City): 'Coriolanus.' Included in *Prefaces to Shakespeare* volume II (Princeton 1947).

1943-4   F.P. Wilson (Smith): 'Elizabethan and Jacobean.' Published as *Elizabethan and Jacobean* (Clarendon 1945).

1944-5   F.O. Matthiessen (Harvard): 'Henry James: the Final Phase.' Published as *Henry James, the Major Phase* (Oxford 1944).

1945-6   Samuel C. Chew (Bryn Mawr): 'The Virtues Reconciled: A Comparison of Visual and Verbal Imagery.' Published as *The Virtues Reconciled, an Iconographical Study* (University of Toronto Press 1947).

1946-7   Marjorie Hope Nicolson (Columbia): 'Voyages to the Moon.' Published as *Voyages to the Moon* (Macmillan 1948).

1947-8   G.B. Harrison (Queen's): 'Shakespearean Tragedy.' Included in *Shakespeare's Tragedies* (Routledge
and Kegan Paul 1951).

1948-9   E.M.W. Tillyard (Cambridge): 'Shakespeare's
Problem Plays.' Published as *Shakespeare's Problem
Plays* (University of Toronto Press 1949).

1949-50   E.K. Brown (Chicago): 'Rhythm in the Novel.'
Published as *Rhythm in the Novel* (University of Toronto Press 1950).

1950-1   Malcolm W. Wallace (Toronto): 'English Character
and the English Literary Tradition.' Published as
English Character and the English Literary Tradition
(University of Toronto Press 1952).

1951-2   R.S. Crane (Chicago): 'The Languages of Criticism
and the Structure of Poetry.' Published as *The
Languages of Criticism and the Structure of Poetry*
(University of Toronto Press 1953).

1952-3   V.S. Pritchett, lectures not given.

1953-4   F.M. Salter (Alberta): 'Mediaeval Drama in Chester.' Published as *Mediaeval Drama in Chester* (University of Toronto Press 1955).

1954-5   Alfred Harbage (Harvard): 'Theatre for Shakespeare.' Published as *Theatre for Shakespeare* (University of Toronto Press 1955).

1955-6   Leon Edel (New York): 'Literary Biography.' Published as *Literary Biography* (University of Toronto
Press 1957).

1956-7   James Sutherland (London): 'On English Prose.'
Published as *On English Prose* (University of Toronto Press 1957).

1957-8   Harry Levin (Harvard): 'The Question of Hamlet.'
Published as *The Question of Hamlet* (Oxford 1959).

1958-9   Bertrand H. Bronson (California): 'In Search of
Chaucer.' Published as *In Search of Chaucer* (University of Toronto Press 1960).

1959-60 Geoffrey Bullough (London): 'Mirror of Minds: Changing Psychological Assumptions as reflected in English Poetry.' Published as *Mirror of Minds: Changing Psychological Beliefs in English Poetry* (University of Toronto Press 1962).

1960-1 Cecil Bald (Chicago): 'The Poetry of John Donne.' Included in *John Donne: A Life* (Oxford 1970).

1961-2 Helen Gardner (Oxford): 'Paradise Lost.' Published as *A Reading of Paradise Lost* (Oxford 1965).

1962-3 Maynard Mack (Yale): 'The Garden and The City: The Theme of Retirement in Pope.' Published as *The Garden and the City* (University of Toronto Press 1969).

1963-4 M.H. Abrams (Cornell): 'Natural Supernaturalism: Idea and Design in Romantic Poetry.' Published as *Natural Supernaturalism* (W.H. Norton 1900).

1964-5 Herschel Baker (Harvard): 'The Race of Time: Three Lectures on Renaissance Historiography.' Published as *The Race of Time* (University of Toronto Press 1967).

1965-6 Northrop Frye (Toronto): 'Fools of Time: Studies in Shakespearian Tragedy.' Published as *Fools of Time* (University of Toronto Press 1967).

1967-8 Frank Kermode (Bristol): 'Criticism and English Studies.' Not published.

1967-8 Francis E. Mineka (Cornell): 'The Uses of Literature, 1750-1850.' Not published.

1968-9 H.D.F. Kitto (Bristol): 'What is Distinctively Hellenic in Greek Literature?' Not published.

1968-9 W.J. Bate (Harvard): 'The Burden of the Past and the English Poet (1660-1840).' Not published.

1970-1 J.A.W. Bennett (Cambridge): 'Chaucer at Oxford and at Cambridge.' Published as *Chaucer at Oxford and at Cambridge* (University of Toronto Press 1974).

1971-2   Roy Daniells (British Columbia): 'Mannerism: An inclusive Art Form.' Not published.

1972-3   Hugh Kenner (California): 'The Meaning of Rhyme.' Not published.

1973-4   Ian Watt (Stanford): 'Four Western Myths.' Publication forthcoming.

1974-5   Richard Ellmann (Oxford): 'The Consciousness of Joyce.' Published as *The Consciousness of Joyce* (Oxford 1977).

1975-6   Henry Nash Smith (Berkeley): 'Other Dimensions: Hawthorne, Melville, and Twain.' Included in *Democracy and the Novel: Popular Resistance to Classic American Writers* (Oxford 1978).

1976-7   Kathleen Coburn (Toronto): 'Some Perspectives on Coleridge.' Published as *Experience into Thought: Perspectives in the Coleridge Notebooks* (University of Toronto Press 1979).

1977-8   E.P. Thompson (Worcester): 'William Blake: Tradition and Revolution 1789-1793.' Publication forthcoming.

1978-9   Ronald Paulson (Yale): 'The Representation of Revolution 1789-1820.' Published as *The Representation of Revolution (1789-1820)* (Yale 1983).

1979-80 David Daiches (Edinburgh): 'Literature and Gentility in Scotland.' Published as *Literature and Gentility in Scotland* (Edinburgh 1982).

1980-1   Walter Ong SJ (St Louis): 'Hopkins, Self and God.' Publication forthcoming.

1982   Robertson Davies (Toronto): 'The Mirror of Nature.' Published as *The Mirror of Nature* (University of Toronto Press 1983).

This book

was designed by

ANTJE LINGNER

of University of

Toronto

Press